Effective Interviewing and Information Gathering

Effective Interviewing and Information Gathering

Proven Tactics to Improve Your Questioning Skills

Thomas Diamante, PhD

Effective Interviewing and Information Gathering: Proven Tactics to Improve Your Questioning Skills
Copyright © Business Expert Press, LLC, 2013.
All rights reserved. No part of this publication may be reproduced, stored in a retrieval system, or transmitted in any form or by any meanselectronic, mechanical, photocopy, recording, or any other except for brief quotations, not to exceed 400 words, without the prior permission of the publisher.

First published in 2013 by
Business Expert Press, LLC
222 East 46th Street, New York, NY 10017
www.businessexpertpress.com

ISBN-13: 978-1-60649-436-3 (paperback)
ISBN-13: 978-1-60649-437-0 (e-book)

Business Expert Press Human Resource Management and Organizational Behavior collection

Collection ISSN: 1946-5637 (print)
Collection ISSN: 1946-5645 (electronic)

Cover and interior design by Exeter Premedia Services Private Ltd., Chennai, India

First edition: 2013

10 9 8 7 6 5 4 3 2 1

Printed in the United States of America.

The joy of life resides in the experiences we create. For my wife, Catherine and my daughters, Nicole and Lauren, three lifelong experiences that create joy for me, all the time.

Abstract

This book is an invaluable, instructional field manual for any professional who needs to obtain and interpret information gathered directly by and from people, without recourse to a technological intermediary, such as online search. In the role of interviewer, interrogator, or evaluator, there are many opportunities to get it wrong. Good information can go bad … bad information can go good, but for the wrong reasons. Either way, without an understanding of process and context, free-standing information runs the risk of sending one in the wrong direction. As advanced as our information-gathering technology may be, it is still impossible to get inside the head of an interviewee by conducting a Google search; so hit them with the tactics spelled out in this book instead in order to protect yourself from being sent in the wrong direction.

Effective Interviewing and Information Gathering Techniques offers the reader a practical introduction to all aspects of obtaining and evaluating information. It serves as a tool-kit that helps build the skills necessary for conducting good interviews and extracting information that is critical for the enterprise in which the interviewer is engaged. As readers progress throughout the book they will acquire an understanding of research-based behavioral techniques that bolster the success rate of interviews. In addition, the legal factors one needs to be aware of prior to conducting an interview for hiring purposes are spelled out. Readers will learn how to design the interview protocol and navigate the murky waters of the give and take involved in gaining access to and interpreting the information found during an interview. Finally, readers will acquire the skills necessary to help them evaluate interview information so that decisions made are based on evidence.

Keywords

executive coaching, assessment, interviewing, information, legal and regulatory, validity, EEO, information gathering, decision making, deception, selection, hiring, succession planning, human capital management

Contents

Foreword xi
Acknowledgments xiii
List of Contributors xv
A Note to Readers—Complementing Research with Practice xvii

Section I   Know Your Destination, Map Your Path,
             and Travel Well 1

Section II   Interact, Discover, and Reflect 39

Section III Uncover, Reveal, and Authenticate 73

Section IV   The Inference Is the Difference 117

Index 141

Foreword

The interview is perhaps the most widely used technique for making selection and promotion decisions. Indeed, anyone involved in hiring someone, regardless of the organizational level or type of job, is likely to conduct an interview. This book is for anyone who relies on the interview to make smarter decisions of various kinds, which means almost anyone in the world of work.

When most of us conduct an interview, we have a variety of information available about the job candidates. We have a resume with a host of background information about prior work experience, education, and skills. We may have recommendations, reference checks, and test scores. However, the interview is usually the clincher; it's the method we use to make the final decision. Sometimes it's the only substantial information we have. Yet interviews are notoriously inaccurate. Simply put, we are not good judges of other people. Our first impressions are especially likely to be wrong. We would do better to flip a coin than rely on an interview. However, would you hire someone sight unseen? Probably not. I wouldn't.

We rely on the interview in part because we believe we are good judges of people. Also, the interview gives us confidence in the person we select. It allows us to be sure we feel comfortable working with the individual. Of course, this might be a biased decision. For instance, we may like someone who is similar to us in ways that have little to do with hiring the best person for the job.

This book is an invaluable set of guidelines for helping us prepare to conduct an interview and being sure that our judgments are as accurate as possible. Thomas Diamante has asked leading practitioners to offer their insights and advice based on research and years of experience. Since we are all going to use the interview as a prime method of making judgments and since we all want to make the best decision possible, we need this book. It shows us how to increase the value of the interview and avoid bias that leads to wrong, and possibly illegal, decisions.

This is as comprehensive and readable set of guidelines you will find anywhere. Each guideline offers clear ideas, vivid examples, and precise behaviors you can use to be sure you are ready to be an interviewer. If you are an experienced interviewer, this will be a useful refresher and a golden resource to have at your side. If you are preparing for your first interview, this will be an invaluable source of ideas and steps to follow to be sure you are ready.

Dr. Diamante is an experienced, licensed industrial and organizational psychologist with training in clinical psychology. He has years of experience as a human resource executive and consultant for major businesses and many nonprofits. He and the authoritative sources who contributed to this volume offer advice on all facets of the interview and information gathering. The guidelines address legal considerations, preparing for the interview, setting the environment to make candidates comfortable, taking notes, paying attention to your own and the interviewee's nonverbal behavior, and using the information to make decisions, to name a few of the topics. You will learn what to ask, how to ask it, how to build rapport, and how to record and process the information. You can read this book in sequence, or peruse the book, dipping into areas of interest or issues that you find confusing. This book hits the topics that most of us find ambiguous or don't think much about but should. In short, you won't find a more practical book anywhere.

Manuel London, PhD
Stony Brook University

Acknowledgments

It is as a result of the science, the practice, and the professionalism represented by this list of contributors that I was able to create this book. I thank each and every one of them for their advice and laser-like ability to nail down what is practical and what is not. These contributors kept an eye on science and an eye on pragmatism so that actionable intelligence resulted.

List of Contributors

Kevin Colwell, PhD
Associate Professor, Psychology
Southern Connecticut State University

Edward R. DelGaizo, PhD
Director, Learning & Development–KPMG
Stony Brook University–College of Business

Steve DiSchiavi
Former Homicide Detective–New York Police Department

Phil Ferrara, PhD
Personnel Manager (Ret.)
United States Unified Court System &
New York University at Polytechnic Institute

Ilene F. Gast, PhD
Senior Research Psychologist
Department of Homeland Security
U.S. Customs and Border Protection

Mort Kissen, PhD
Clinical Professor
Derner Institute for Advanced Psychological Studies

Jennifer Pelt Wisdom, PhD, MPH
Associate Professor, Psychiatry,
Columbia University College of Physicians and Surgeons
Research Scientist, New York State Psychiatric Institute

Georges Ramalanjaona, MD, DSc, MBA
Clinical Associate Adjunct Professor of Emergency Medicine
Touro College of Osteopathic Medicine, NY
Director of Medical Education
St John's Episcopal Hospital, Department of Emergency Medicine

John C. Scott, PhD
Chief Operating Officer
APTMetrics, Inc.

Joyce Silberstang, PhD
Department of Management, Marketing & Decision Sciences
Adelphi University–School of Business

A Note to Readers—Complementing Research with Practice

This book is an instructional field manual for any professional who needs to access and interpret information from people and not technology. As the interviewer, questioner, or evaluator we face many opportunities to get it wrong.

Good information can go bad when you don't interpret it correctly. Bad information can go good, incorrectly sending you in the wrong direction.

You can't Google the head of the person you are interviewing, so hit them with evidence-based tactics that will give you the information you want. The Action Items in this book will help you do just that. The action items are based on sound, empirical research converted into practical ways to improve questioning skills. The action items are both empirically important and practically useful.

The thrust of this book is focused on improving interviewing skills for the sake of (1) ensuring that legal/regulatory concerns governing the employment interview become nonconcerns, (2) enhancing access to information that might otherwise be difficult to unearth, and (3) ensuring that due diligence is done so that information is evaluated in a way that will lead to making better decisions. The guidelines in this book are advisory and reflect the advice of leading authorities and research.

In my 25 years of cross-industry human resource and business experience, assessing people for a wide variety of reasons, I've learned what many skilled interviewers already know. The intangibles present during dialogue are rich and rewarding avenues for discovery. To realize benefits from this, we need to be both structured in our approach to interviewing and nimble so we can fully utilize whatever comes our way. We can and should plan but we also need to think (and respond) on our feet.

This book offers guidelines to ensure objectivity, standardization, and structure. However, structuring an interview protocol does not negate the value of learning to be open, inquisitive, and skilled in dissecting intangibles that lead to value-added information. The thrust of the book is focused on interviewing for hiring, promotion, and succession planning. For clarity, Section III offers action items useful for information gathering in general, not necessarily as only instruction for employment interviewing *per se*. It is in this section that interviewers are offered best practices from all kinds of skilled interviewers from various settings.

The reader is also advised to read each section with an eye toward optimizing information gathered during any assessment context. Many action items transcend use of the interview to assess job fit alone and generalize to other uses such as executive coaching, psychological assessments, interrogations, and identification of high potential employees for leadership positions.

What do people say when they don't talk? What is it that people tell you, despite the words they use? How do you make sense of all this in a way that improves the value of the information you collect? This book will allow you to better understand what someone says, even when they are saying something different, and understanding what someone says even when not speaking at all.

Knowing how to handle the intangibles or dynamics of the interview is distinct from authoring the content of a question as is dictated throughout this book. Doing both brings exponential value to the process of question asking, information gathering, information evaluation, and ultimately decision making. You simply can't benefit from or utilize information that you can't access. Mining the gray area of intangibles is what separates the good interviewer from the great interviewer.

The book articulates practical advice on how to structure the interview while remaining open as well. This is a powerful combination. Working with the structured (and the unstructured) aspects of an interview yields unfound value. *The action items in this book will equip you to face the interview situation with a plan for the predictable and the competence to handle and benefit from the unpredictable.*

This book will improve your ability to ask questions. It will do this by incorporating the objective and intangible elements that define dialogue. Like the beauty of The Royal Ballet or the emotion of a Beethoven symphony, the interview is a dynamic artistic event consisting of structure and nuance. When played well together, structure and nuance produce a rich, dense, full tonality that enables truth. The action items in this book will improve your questioning skills and turn you into an *interview artisan*.

> *"Not everything that counts can be counted,*
> *and not everything that can be counted counts."*
> —Einstein

SECTION I

Know Your Destination, Map Your Path, and Travel Well

This section addresses preparation for the interview process for recruitment and selection. To be prepared to interview effectively, you must understand the job, tasks being performed, and individual characteristics that will lead to success on the job. Then, you must create an interview protocol that has consistent structured questions that will assess the characteristics required to be excellent. Additionally, you must create a clear and objective scoring key that focuses on behaviors rather than subjective judgments. Finally, you must plan to document the content of the interview using objective, behavioral terms removing (as best possible) subjectivity in interpreting and understanding what the interviewee reported. It is advised that your scoring key be anchored with objective, behavioral statements. In fact, mapping interview content to ratings or evaluations that are anchored or defined by job-related, behavioral statements secures "reliability" (consistency) among interviewers, an important ingredient in defending the "validity" (i.e., accurate and job-related nature) of the interview ratings.

The technical term "validity" means that the content of the interview is job-related, objective, and behavioral in nature. Legal and regulatory guidelines demand validity when a business needs to defend its use of the interview as a selection or promotion tool (or any method, practice, or procedure that affects the employment status of an individual). A valid interview is one that measures what it purports to measure and that predicts what it is supposed to predict. Structure enables objectivity and validity. A valid interview is structured, standardized, and job-related.

You will see the word "reliable" in literature on assessment and interviewing (and in this book). Reliability should not be confused with validity. Reliable means the assessment is consistent—but not necessarily consistently right. Validity means it is both consistent and accurate. As an example, a dart that misses its target but hits the exact same place every time is reliable. One that hits the bull's eye consistently is not only reliable but also valid (accurate). We want interview processes and outcomes to be both reliable (consistent) and valid (accurate). In fact, you can't have validity without reliability (though you can have reliability without validity). By far, structured, job-related interviews are always a wise way to go. And learning how to handle the dynamics that percolate during dialogue will enhance the value of the interview process.

All hiring and promotion interviews are considered a type of selection test or tool (i.e., a method used to make human resource decisions), and thus they need to be sensitive to, if not deferential toward, legal and regulatory standards. Accordingly, it is necessary to ensure that a careful, systematic, and evidence-based effort is undertaken to understand the required tasks, knowledge, skill, ability, and other characteristics required to effectively perform a particular job or role. This is the domain of competency modeling and job analysis.

Although necessary and legally required, there are many challenges to conducting a thorough job analysis. It can be time consuming and expensive to do a detailed job analysis and by the time the analysis is complete, the job itself could change because of the turbulent business and economic challenge coupled with emerging technologies that change how organizations and roles in organizations operate constantly. In fact, the shelf-life of job roles and responsibilities seems to shorten all the time. As business models adapt to global competition, emerging technologies, and dynamic consumer demands, so too do job requirements change. So job analysis work is now challenged by this fluidity.

For some, it may feel as if stating a job requirement is like taking a snapshot to capture the movement of a speeding car. The onus is on the human resources professional to ensure that competencies (i.e., knowledge, skills, abilities, and personal characteristics) required for success are defined—and that context of the job situation is taken into consideration. The fact that change is constant necessitates even more the need to ensure that selection and promotion decisions be grounded in sound practice and knowledge of what the business needs to be successful.

Change or constant adaptation can't be a convenient excuse for making bad decisions (i.e., decisions that are not based on valid practices).

Regardless of the challenges, it is never appropriate to ignore or overlook the process of conducting an effective and valid job analysis because it is the foundation for creating an effective, reliable, and valid structured interview protocol. Anything short of this is a waste of time. Explaining how to conduct an effective, efficient, and valid job analysis is beyond the scope of this book. The interested reader is referred to other good sources of information on job analysis such as O*Net Online (http://www.onetonline.org/) and the Office of Personnel Management (http://www.opm.gov) guidance on human capital management, specifically assessment and selection. That being said, the need for a legal defense of a selection procedure (including an interview) should always be assumed and evidentiary preparation is advised (http://www.uniformguidelines.com/uniformguidelines.html).

1. Action Item

Know the challenge in the job before you know the person.

Rationale

The goal of an employment interview is to assess a candidate's ability to do the job well. Therefore, the interview needs to assess the extent to which the candidate has the skills, abilities, knowledge, motivation, and other characteristics required by the job. So, design the interview process based on knowledge of the challenge, job, or opportunity for which you are conducting the assessment.

Distinguish between technical competencies (i.e., skills and knowledge) and nontechnical competencies (abilities, values, interests, personal characteristics). Both can be important, but for different reasons.

Do your homework before you construct the interview protocol:

- What are the demands of the job or situation?
- What is unique or distinctive about this opportunity (compared with jobs or opportunities like this elsewhere)?

- What differentiates exceptional performance from average performance?
- What causes poor performance?
- What does success look like?
- What characteristics do successful people possess?
- What does failure look like? What causes failure?
- What characteristics do poor performers possess?

Dissect job requirements into critical incidents, that is, articulate what will "make or break performance." Interview content will be shaped by questions that matter most in the prediction of good and bad behavior on the job—go after what causes success and what results in derailment. Collect examples of critical incidents and pay attention to poor performance and high performance indicators. This is so because the factors that cause poor performance or failure can be different from the factors that cause high performance. You want to know them both.

For example, an individual may be able to perform a task when no time pressure exists; however, under pressure, derailment might occur. It is important to incorporate the context of critical job incidents into the interview process. For example, "Tell me about a time when you were able to turn-around an organization under a harshly demanding deadline—what did you do, how did you do it, and what was the outcome? Did you create a positive, measureable impact on the business? How did you assess that?" This question is not the same question as "Tell me your thoughts about being a turn-around agent."

Not to be stereotypical but, other examples include being technically competent for a position yet nontechnical competencies are so lacking that failure exists. A practical example of this is seen when professionals deep in technical acumen (e.g., medical doctors, information technology professionals, and doctoral level researchers) are promoted to management positions and then suddenly the wheels fall off as weak interpersonal skills get displayed and they fail to engage, activate, and motivate their business units. Success as an independent contributor or "technician" is not the same as getting things done through others. It is important to learn what causes success and failure in a job so that the interview can tap into the human elements that will predict overall performance.

It's important to know what makes people successful as well as what makes them unsuccessful. Answers to questions such as these can be realized using job analysis, conducting reviews of the literature in journals associated with the candidate's profession, direct observation of current employees, and interviewing subject matter experts. Court cases have established that systematic analysis of job requirements is necessary to establish the job appropriateness of any given interview (or selection) protocol, so it is important to thoroughly analyze the job and document the procedures used to determine job relevance of any assessed characteristic.

It is worth noting that when screening tools (i.e., interview, written tests, a "scored" or evaluated work sample or performance of any kind) do *not* produce an "adverse impact" (i.e., statistical disparity between majority and minority group members) or if the interviewer does not blatantly mistreat candidates or create the perception of mistreatment (i.e., "adverse treatment") then the need for evidentiary documentation is not great. However, one is hard-pressed to see a basis for asking questions blindly—that is without an understanding of what will predict job performance and so a job analysis of some sort is always advised. One is equally hard-pressed to find a rationale for not providing the interviewer guidance so that they gain access to the information that will be useful to them in making decisions. On the legal front, the focus is to make sure that everyone is treated fairly—equal opportunity—unfair or illegal bias does not affect decisions. On the business and decision-making front the focus is on drawing inferences that predict success. We can have our cake and eat it too.

"It is o.k. to be fairly stupid as long as you are stupid fairly" is a well-worn phrase known in the selection profession. This means that legally you are not at risk if your interview practices do not differentially impact protected classes of people (i.e., gender, race, national origin, ethnicity, and religious affiliation). That is, if everyone experiences a useless interview and are subject to misjudgments based on bad (but not illegal) sources of information, then legally it's okay.

But ... why in the world would anyone waste time and effort to conduct a useless interview? Of course, no one does so intentionally. But the legal benchmarks and the professional knowledge available to drive good information collection and use march to different drummers.

Said differently, it is not illegal to create a bad (subjective, unstructured, not job-related) interview as long as it treats everyone equally badly. It is not illegal to destroy your organization by hiring and promoting ill-equipped people. It is not illegal to hire someone who will likely fail at the job. It's just asinine.

So, do the hard work. Analyze the job. Determine what causes success and failure. Be thorough. Realize that different elements can lead to both success and failure and then connect your interview questions to job requirements.

Learn the requirements, the demands of the challenge, or the expectations of the challenge. Are deadlines severe? Is timing critical? Is performance individually driven or a consequence of getting others to work together effectively? Are global issues relevant? Are these demands cross-cultural, cross-organizational, or both?

What are the consequences of failure? Factor in context—what are the stakes if failure occurs? Do people lose lives or only money? Are others placed in danger based on performance? Will mistakes negatively affect the public, fellow employees, or perhaps corporate reputation?

You will use this analysis to develop interview questions, simulations, and other assessment methods that are credible in the eyes of the candidate and valid in terms of job-relatedness.

Capture the context and consequences of work performed. There is a difference between walking on a 5-inch-wide plank of wood resting on the floor and doing the same from 10 stories high to rescue a child on the other end of the plank. Context matters.

2. Action Item

Set the stage in order to sample behaviors in the proper context.

Rationale

State why you are meeting and what you hope to accomplish. Formulate questions in advance. Don't leave this to the last minute. Embrace your goal—why are you conducting the interview? Why an interview and not a questionnaire? Why not just meet on the web? Enter the interview knowing why you are deploying your chosen method. Is this interview going to require emotion from the interviewer or the interviewee? Are you prepared for that? Is the interview a cold, business-like question/answer scenario? If so, are your questions and potential answers on which to assess or score the responses objective (using behavioral anchors) and standardized (to ensure consistency)?

Social settings impact behavior in general and during the interview in particular. Advise the interviewee of the proper context to clarify even if you think it is or should be obvious. Sometimes the signals get crossed and the result is an inaccurate assessment.

For example, due to logistics, candidates for senior management jobs for a Big Four Consulting firm were interviewed at a resort. The relaxed setting did not mirror the intensity and importance of the interview and this fact was stated up-front. A candidate assuming that the resort setting calls for a relaxed style dressed casually and spoke informally. She was sent home on the next flight.

Establish context for the interview up-front. Tell the interviewee what you hope to gain from having this conversation. Inform the candidate about the type of information you want. For example, if you are collecting information about how problems were handled in a prior job, tell the candidate "when you answer please try to give me the details, telling me exactly what you did and how you did it." If you want them to respond to a simulated work question or engage in a role play, inform them of this up-front. "I'd like to ask you to analyze a business case. I'd like you to approach the work problem just as if we were working on the case together."

Failure to inform the interviewee about what you expect of them can confuse the situation leading to the collection of insufficient, inaccurate, or incomplete information. Incorrect inferences are often drawn during evaluations because the interviewee simply did not understand what was expected of them.

For example, if it is a selection interview, set the agenda for what types of questions will be asked, how much time you have, and what level of details you expect. Tell the candidate "I will make sure we have ample time for you to ask questions of me near the end of the interview"—"We only have 30 minutes so if you don't mind, we need to move rapidly through the questions, if you can be blunt and crisp that would help"—"This interview will require that I ask you some personal questions about your life and work and values. While I do not ordinarily just ask people these types of questions before getting to know them, in this circumstance we only have about 90 minutes together and I want to learn as much as I can about you. So, please excuse me for treading on areas and asking questions about past events that are either upsetting or difficult or both." Stating instructions like this demonstrates courtesy, respect, and it is also very practical.

Some interview situations where setting the stage is very useful:

- when the interview is part of a larger review or selection practice and time is short
- when the stakes are very high for the candidate and the decision maker (e.g., placement decisions in high-risk occupations or mission-critical assignments)
- when the need to probe about the causes of past success and failure is important, perhaps as follow-up to information already received through an alternate means
- when the interview is a follow-up to an initial interview and the nature of the questions are more challenging, more complex, and more difficult to answer

3. Action Item

Ask questions that differentiate people.

Rationale

Prepare and deliver questions in a way that will maximize the likelihood that the candidates will *express themselves.*

Enabling access to the "true person" you are interviewing requires the skill of a good comedian—knowing what to say, when to say it, and how to say it—to optimize the response. Question content is key and should be a derivative of a job analysis, or other systematic analysis to ensure relevance of question content.

Question content should make it likely that you can distinguish people based on their responses. Otherwise, your day is spent collecting information that brings you no level of distinction between the interviewees you met. While question content is a key tool, delivery of that content is the artistry of the excellent interviewer.

Remain focused on what you ask, how you ask it, and when. You need to be consistent in the questions asked and in your interactions with candidates but, at the same time, you must be responsive to the situation and the candidate. Ask yourself the following questions before you ask the interviewee anything.

- What is the best style to use for this candidate?
  - A style that mirrors the candidate to optimize comfort and reduce defenses.
- Do I have concerns about potential defensiveness?
  - Overcome potential resistance through respect, demeanor, and lobbing over soft questions before you challenge.
- How can I get the candidate to show me qualities I need to know?
  - Being empathetic, display understanding, and share some personal anecdotes or even failure if you want to extract similar stories from others.
- When should I ask questions that are personally, cognitively, or emotionally challenging?
  - Ask when rapport is evident and introduce a "warm-up" question before you strike.

4. Action Item

Ask employment interview questions by first stating the relevant job requirement and then ask a question addressing that requirement.

Rationale

Legal reviews, federal guidelines, and professional standards along with empirical research all point in the direction that "valid" or accurate selection practices are "best" built on the basis of job requirements. Traditionally, this requires a job analysis. Professional and federal regulations remain relevant regarding the importance of understanding the job in question before interviewing to fill it. At a practical level, organizations can go far by advising that employment interviewers be able to begin an interview question with a summary or description of essential, job requirements (or competencies) that are core for the job or job family.

The value of this tactic is that (a) the job candidate is focused on the fact that the question is fair, legitimate, and job relevant, (b) the interviewer is focused on inferring the relevancy of the candidate's answer with respect to a specific requirement of the job as it relates to the business environment, and (c) the simplicity of the tactic satisfies fundamental, expected interview structure stipulated in professional and regulatory guidelines mitigating against wrong, unlawful personnel decisions while bringing the best-qualified individual to the job. Finally, it is a tactic that can be embraced by line management, it is easy to follow, and its value to the organization is self-evident.

It is important to focus on the competency (or skill or ability) that is essential for success. The stem of the question can begin with a statement of the requirement followed by a question that naturally connects to that demand. A very simple tactic that can be deployed is to phrase your employment questions in the following way, "The job requires xyz, please tell me about a time when you (or how would you go about) …" There should be a clear and direct connection between the job requirement and your request for information about what the candidate did in the past or would do in the future that relates to the stem of your query.

5. Action Item

Structure the process and the content of the interview.

Rationale

The architecture of the interview is critical. Lack of clarity or ill-defined expectations may lead to poor judgments, inappropriate responses (time spent, length, level of detail), and other contaminating factors by the interviewer, interviewee, or both.

The interview should have a beginning. What is the purpose of the interview? How much time is allotted? What will be the nature of the questions? Is there an expectation for brevity or eloquence? Details or generalities? Formality or informality?

The interview content should be stated. This prompts memory early, saves time, and begins to place the interviewee on track. This informs the interviewee about priorities.

Lack of structure invites error from many sources, compromising the value of the interview. Error comes from the lack of structure. Lack of structure can also spawn confusion among interviewers who find themselves in a morass of candidates and questions without a clear path or standardization from which to compare interview findings.

Structure imposes discipline, focus, and validity (i.e., accuracy). Write questions that are job related. Define the interview so that all candidates experience the same interview content. Articulate a means to measure responses across candidates using the same metrics or means of evaluating the "goodness" or "badness" of a response. Write these metrics in a way that anyone can easily interpret them—make them as concrete or objective as possible. Anchor ratings or evaluations in behavioral terminology (i.e., objective indicators of past behavior and/or specifics of how a situation was analyzed or addressed).

Avoid subjectivity by describing the contents of a good answer and bad answer. This is best accomplished by describing behavior or actions. For instance, "the candidate appears hungry" is not as good as "the candidate got up and ate a cookie." All interviewers would likely agree on the observed behavior. Having all interviewers ask the same questions enables comparisons across candidate responses.

Poor calibration of benchmarks, standardization, or metrics invites biases both covert and overt in the evaluation of the candidate's responses. Structure interview data collection so that you can capture what the person says or did and why or how they did it. Offer the interviewer the tools necessary to compare and evaluate the results.

An important practical consideration—

Please note that the structured interviewer can be viewed as robotic; so it is important to retain a personality despite delivering a planned set of questions. Close the interview by reflecting on the nature of the dialogue. Show respect and appreciation for the interviewee's time. Do this always.

6. Action Item

Use clearly defined scoring standards to evaluate responses to interview questions.

Rationale

Regardless of the nature or purpose of an interview, it is essential that interviewers have at their disposal a set of scoring standards that predefine the criteria for evaluating responses to the questions. The purpose of these standards is to establish a reliable means for judging an interviewee's standing on the dimension being measured. Additionally, these standards serve to "calibrate" assessors' judgments so that all interviewees are evaluated using the same standards regardless of the assessor.

Behavioral evaluation standards should be developed for each dimension that is to be assessed through the interview (e.g., interpersonal skills). Evaluation standards are most useful when presented in the form of behavioral statements. Behaviorally based evaluation standards reflect observable and verifiable actions. Oftentimes referred to as behavioral "anchors," these standards guide the interviewer's evaluation by clearly delineating the acceptability of responses along an effectiveness continuum on the dimension being measured. Behavioral anchors can be developed from the information obtained in the job analysis. The behavioral anchors rest on the actions or deeds or observables that separate great, good, and not so good (bad) performance.

Interview dimensions that are defined along an effectiveness continuum are better understood by when anchors exist and this improves interviewer judgment.

For example:

"Tell me about a time when you led a business unit that had a mission-critical objective. Explain the nature of the impact of the unit and describe how you leveraged your team to accomplish the objective."

The response to the preceding question could be evaluated using the following anchored rating scale for the head of a business unit:

- (5) ***Exceeding***: Significantly improved team performance over the course of the year by establishing challenging goals, promoting cooperation and team spirit, and encouraging participative planning and decision making, tangible outcomes exist based on leveraging competencies of others.
- (3) ***Fully Performing***: Solicited team members' ideas and opinions and utilized these to make plans and decisions, delegated effectively based on competencies, some but not all business outcomes exist.
- (1) ***Not Meeting***: Expended much effort overcoming rudimentary conflicts among team members, resorted to doing much work independent of the team, business outcomes failed to be realized.

Since behavioral anchors are so crucial to the accurate measurement of interview performance, it is necessary to apply a rigorous approach to their development and implementation. Specifically, evaluation standards need to be validated to ensure that they accurately describe performance expectations for each characteristic being measured by the interview. In addition, these standards need to be appropriately calibrated so that they accurately delineate candidate responses along an effectiveness continuum.

Best practice in developing behavioral anchors is to establish them based on subject matter experts. These experts are people who do, have done, and/or supervise the job for which anchors are being established. Behavioral or objective anchors guard against subjectivity and "error" in the process of judging or evaluating the meaning of what was said during the interview.

7. Action Item

Know the value of various answers before you get them.

Rationale

What good is a question if it doesn't lead to an answer that is meaningful or fails to carve a path to more useful information?

Construct questions and potential answers. In formalized or evaluative scenarios, your questions should sample or probe a characteristic of the person whether it is a knowledge, skill, ability, or other characteristic (in today's vernacular these are referred to as "competencies"). You pose a question for a reason. Know the reason and factor this into a "structured guide" so you can score or metric the response you receive. Do this in advance of data collection, else you risk polluting the value of the information you access due to misinterpretation, poor inferences, or failures of judgment.

Technical know-how or competencies can easily be assessed in such a manner as well. On the basis of subject matter experts, excellent, good, and poor answers to technical questions can be generated in advance. Think of this as reverse engineering the interview dialogue.

When information gathered is a lead or means to access other information, create "linking maps"—essentially these maps will link one piece of information (or door opener) to another piece of information. Do this before and not after you collect information to enhance the power of the information you collect and remain on the right path. This path can serve as a compass to all those involved in investigating, probing, and connecting—and, most importantly, it keeps the user of information close to factual, objective evidence, removing personal, interpersonal, or other elements that, in this instance, may have no relevance. The largest source of error comes from subjectivity embedded in poor questions, poor evaluative benchmarks, and/or the interviewer's needs, motives, and personality. Protect yourself from yourself by using structured tools for valuation of the interviewee.

Beware the interview protocol mistake of stacking questions that do not distinguish one interviewee from another. If the goal of our interview process is to measure or distinguish one candidate from another, then questions that do not lead to differentiation are useful. To test on the utility of the interview, monitor the evaluations at the end of the interview. You should see noticeable differences in how interviewees stack up based on the anchors used to judge them.

8. Action Item

Minimize the risk of legal or regulatory violations (Equal Employment Opportunity).[1]

Rationale

Interviews are legally challenged for three main reasons: poor questions, subjectivity, and inconsistent application or administration. Questions that are not job-related or that *appear* discriminatory in intent are more likely to be successfully challenged by candidates than those that are clearly related to the requirements of the job.

Best practice calls for a structured interview design whereby the questions and scoring standards follow a formal outline and are determined in advance of the interview. With this approach, every candidate is asked the same set of questions and their responses are scored against the same set of criteria. Furthermore, properly designed, structured interview questions target only those characteristics that are critical for job success.

Some good examples:

> "The position we seek to fill calls for integrating two organizations that have been operating independent of each other. We are certain that integration will yield enormous business advantages. Can you tell me about how you would approach such a task?"

---

[1]. The Uniform Guidelines is a critical document used by attorneys, courts, and assessment professionals to guide, if not, evaluate the "validity" or adequacy (i.e., business necessity and job-relatedness) of a selection procedure or human resource decision-making tool or process. (http://uniformguidelines.com/uniformguidelines.html)

"One key responsibility in this role is to deal with senior management on matters that are emotionally difficult, usually very sensitive in nature and often could lead to litigious activity if mishandled. Can you tell me about your experience handling such circumstances and please do tell me exactly the nature of the circumstance, what you did to handle it, and how it resolved?"

"This role is a leadership role to take a failing organization and make it successful. We need to turn the organization around. Sales are dropping and competition is fierce. Please share with us what you did in the past in similar situations. Tell us the industry, inform us about internal and external pressures you needed to face, and offer us what you believe led to either success or failure in that turnaround role?"

This necessary link between interview questions and job requirements is accomplished through a formal validation study, which documents the job-relatedness of the questions and serves as the foundation for the interview's legal defensibility.

As important as it is to demonstrate the validity or job-relatedness of the interview questions, it is equally important to ensure that the scoring standards are accurately calibrated against the performance expectations of the characteristic being measured. These standards, which should be developed in the form of behavioral statements, need to be carefully scrutinized during the validation process to ensure that the proficiency expectations closely approximate the work situation.

An interviewer who strays from a structured interview protocol can inadvertently ask questions that may be deemed illegal or irrelevant to the job. That is why it is important to stick to the structured interview protocol to avoid asking irrelevant or legally questionable questions.

Some examples of questions, possibly illegal questions, that don't appear illegal at first blush are offered. Often, the interviewer is not intentionally violating law yet he/she is. *Please remember that the impact of what the interviewer says and does is as important as the intent behind what is said and done in terms of interviewing in the employment context. Too many interviewers find themselves being deposed in response to allegations of wrongful discrimination and offering "but I was only trying to make conversation"—so, make conversation about the job and its demands. Stay clear of well-intentioned commentaries that can get you in trouble.* This again is another solid example of why standardizing, structuring, and making sure assessment questions are job-related is a best practice.

Some questions that can be suggestive of unfair (illegal) bias:

Query—"It's important that we help our communities, what clubs do you belong to?"
Problem—touches on interests that could be related to a protected class characteristic or equal opportunity protected characteristic (e.g., disabilities) and so the interviewee might infer that you are judging them and making decisions on the basis of this characteristic—illegal.
Query—"Wow, I see you graduated from a top-tier university, did you enter under a special arrangement?"
Problem—assuming the candidate required a special consideration to enter a top-tier school (rather than assuming it was based on academic achievement) could be inferred to be reflective of a racial, ethnic, religious, gender, or national origin stereotype—inferences drawn on the basis of protected characteristics are illegal.
Query—"It's so hard to balance life and work, I know my wife has real hard time with this, and this job is so demanding, do you think it will be hard on your kids?"
Problem—making the assumption that the candidate cannot perform an essential function of the job because of children is violating Title VII Civil Rights Act (1964, 1991) protecting gender as well as other characteristics.
Comment—"Wow, you really look nice in that interview suit!"
Problem—this is obviously suggestive and has no place in evaluating the individual's competence; gender neutral in delivery, this comment triggers a basis for a discrimination allegation.

Interviewers should ask questions of candidates as to whether they can perform the job and how they would perform it. They should use polite and tactful interruptions when a candidate strays from the original question or brings up issues that could be deemed illegal or irrelevant to the ability to perform the job. Please note that the instruction to structure the interview does not preclude the need to allow freedom of expression or to probe, pause, and persevere when relevant avenues appear.

9. Action Item

Assess only essential characteristics required for successful job performance.

Rationale

As with any technique used to assess candidates for employment decisions, questions should be based on a job analysis that delineates the important knowledge, skills, abilities, and personal characteristics required for success on the job. In fact, the 1978 *Uniform Federal Guidelines on Employee Selection Procedures*[2] advises that selection instruments only measure those factors necessary to perform the work successfully (these guidelines remain relevant).

The criteria for satisfactory job performance must be clearly defined before an interview is developed. While it is not necessary to measure every important characteristic, it is necessary that every characteristic measured be important. A job analysis will drive recommendations for which characteristics to assess, while practical considerations will drive recommendations for how many (and which) of these characteristics to assess.

Once the interview is developed, it is necessary to confirm or validate the questions to be certain that they address critical aspects of the job and relate to the targeted characteristics. This process is typically accomplished through the use of subject matter experts (people who currently perform or supervise the targeted job). Each subject matter expert is asked to evaluate each question and make judgments indicating the extent to which each interview question is essential versus merely useful and whether or not the item can be linked to a substantive element of the

---

2. Courts show great deference to the Uniform Federal Guidelines and it is important to note that any method, practice, or procedure that affects the employment status of an individual can come under the scrutiny of these regulatory guidelines.

job. In addition, it is useful to find out if the characteristic being measured is a requirement on "day one" or whether it is learned over time.

While organizations can decide their own criteria for hire, that is, whether a skill or ability (or competency) is required on day one or whether it can be learned on the job, it is very useful for interviewers to be aware of this so they don't factor in the lack of a skill as a deal breaker when instead that skill can be learned over time. In fact, it is often useful to connect training and development plans to entry requirements so newcomers have a clear path for getting up-to-speed and interviewers are aware of this as well.

Both competencies needed upon hire and competencies to-be developed are therefore very useful to interviewers. Selection criteria should be set squarely on what is necessary upon hire, and other attributes to be learned on the job can be planned for in advance (note: it is perfectly okay to incorporate ability to learn the job into the interview process).

Employment or prescreen interviews also typically include an assessment of minimum qualifications, such as education or experience. It is equally important to validate these qualifications, as they frequently serve as knock-out factors in a screening process. Any and all qualifications should be investigated and validated as a true requirement of the job.

Differences in hiring rates (i.e., selection rates) or "adverse impact" on protected categories or classifications of people can be legally challenged. Validation of your interview supports the business necessity and fairness of your procedures. Qualifications used to make employment decisions must meet the test of being so important that without it, the candidate could not perform the job at even a minimally acceptable level. Any method, practice, or procedure that affects the employment status of the individual (hiring, promotion, termination, and possibly developmental avenues required for advancement) should be validated.

Technical validation practices all rest on the demonstration of being job-related, objective, and standardized (www.siop.org/_**Principles/ principles**default.aspx). Organizations are advised to seek appropriate legal and professional counsel to ensure that validation practices support the human resource tools and practices implemented to make placement decisions, be these interview practices or other assessment means.

10. Action Item

Dissect the advantages gained by panel interviews before implementation.

Rationale

There are many reasons to use a panel of interviewers but in itself it does not bolster the validity of the interview unless you incorporate all the elements necessary in a structured interview. To that effect, the panel becomes useful for many reasons besides the structure itself. Panels are as good as other structured interview approaches but not necessarily better than a single interviewer when they are both behaviorally based structured tools. Panels do provide higher buy-in and participation with those vested in the decision, which is an important consideration outside of the decision and the legality of the interview itself.

Interestingly, in a study that compared panels and individual interviewer scenarios, there was no evidence found of any systematic errors that would attenuate the validity of individual interviewer ratings. On the basis of these results, it was concluded that the individual interviewers were equally capable of making valid predictions about future behavior from interview responses. When structured, both panel and nonpanel interviews can be equally good.

Of particular note is the fact that the interviews in this study were structured and raters were trained prior to its administration. These two elements are critical points. When interview questions are structured and raters are properly trained, multiple interviewers may not bring advantage.

From a legal exposure standpoint, the use of multiple interviewers does not appear to add significant value to the defense of interview results. A review of 99 federal district court cases that examined the relationship between aspects of interview structure and litigation outcomes cases found that the use of multiple interviewers demonstrated a relatively weak relationship with litigation outcomes (see Williamson reference). When interviews are properly designed (e.g., structured, based upon a job analysis, validated), the use of multiple interviewers does not appear to be needed. The results of research indicate that the job-relatedness of the interview is the principal determining factor in the judges' decision. However, to the extent that multiple interviewers bring additional attention and focus to job requirements and also serve to keep each other "on-track" during and after the interview, multiple interviewers practically speaking can be very useful.

It appears that as long as the interview is validated, structured, and contains behaviorally based scoring standards (i.e., is very concrete, objective, or defines terms concretely) and the interviewers are properly trained, panels and individual interviewer approaches are equally good. All these criteria are not always met and consequently multiple interviewers can reduce the risk that questions go in the wrong direction and/or that answers be misinterpreted when the interview is complete.

Eliminating interviewer panels can reduce the cost of assessment and brings logistical ease. However, there may be organizational reasons that make panels advantageous. Most importantly, if the degree of structure, analysis, and validation is weak (or moderate or unknown), the panel offers tremendous advantage over the unstructured interview and the poorly trained individual interviewer. Use the panel in that instance.

11. Action Item

Ask about future and past behavior and be specific.

Rationale

Asking about performance about a specific past behavior forces the candidate to discuss the details around an event. Alternatively, asking about a behavior that might be demonstrated in a hypothetical situation forces the candidate to think about and articulate how they would behave in the future.

Hypothetical questions, referred to as situational interview questions, are highly predictive of performance (i.e., revealing what the person would do, how they would do it, and discussing the rationale driving behavior). Behavioral description interviews (detailing past behavior in specific situations) are also good for assessing experience and competence. Both situational and behavioral description interview questions have been shown to be the most predictive types of interview formats. The choice of focusing on specific past behaviors (behavioral interview) versus focusing on potential behaviors in job-relevant hypothetical situations (situational interview) depends on what you are assessing and, of course, the background of the candidate. As long as the interview is structured and job-related, validity is high.

It is wise to incorporate questions that reveal not only what a person "has done" but also their thoughts and plans about what they "may do" in specific, job-relevant situations. Indeed, there are often circumstances that dictate interviewing an individual for responsibilities they have yet to realize in their career—especially those most relevant for advancement planning (i.e., making investments in continuing to develop the individual for management in general) or deliberate succession planning (i.e., readiness for placement in a specific job). Oftentimes it is wise to tap into existing talent pools (internal candidates) to stretch or grow people even if they do not necessarily show a track record of having done what you hope them to do. However, they do reveal the aptitude to learn and the motivation necessary for success.

As a rule of thumb, if the candidate is able to show that he or she was able to deliver in previous situations, and/or is able to understand how to behave in the hypothetical situation, then it is likely that the person can perform that behavior under the same or similar required circumstances in the future.

Probing past behavior is useful. It is vital to get the specifics. What exactly was the situation? What did you do? Why? Was there an outcome? In this way, the behavioral descriptions are rich in content and the interviewer can make more accurate inferences about the potential to handle similar job-related situations in the future. While the candidate does not offer the exact experience desired, the nature of the challenges and problems they've faced can imply the capability to handle similar situations in the future. So, questions about past behavior and future behavior are useful avenues for assessing competence now and for windows into the potential of the individual to handle specific responsibilities in the future.

Behavior speaks louder than words. Whether you focus on past or future-oriented questions, remain focused on capturing the interviewee's actions. If you have biographical data available, then try to sample from that track record. See the pattern of behaviors that relate to the individual's development (or lack thereof) and ask questions to see if the pattern, style, or characteristic you suspect is present.

- Why did they make the decisions they did?
- How did they make a project successful?
- What was managing the project like on a daily basis?
- What did they actually do to earn buy-in of others?

Interviewee actions over time are a wonderful sample of who they are, where they are going, and why they are headed in that direction. Past behavior can be used to predict future behavior. Elements of past behavior in stated situations can suggest potential for handling similar challenges in the future. Demonstrations of stretching oneself, tackling new responsibilities being open to criticism and learning—all these things can be evidenced by past behavior and are useful for planning the future of the individual. In addition, hypothetical questions too can lend insight into what a person what or could do when confronting a defined challenge in the future.

A quick summary:

Behavioral descriptions are captured by questions such as:

"When you faced the possibility that the irate resident might cause you physical harm, what did you do? What were you thinking? How did you handle it? What was the outcome?"

"Tell me about a time when you were faced with a business problem that required you to compromise the quality of your work in order to meet a deadline. What was the problem? What compromise did you make? How did you feel about making that compromise?"

Situational responses are enabled by questions such as:

"How would you handle an employee who reports to you whose work quality has been falling below your expectations for the past three months?"

"Imagine a time when you are trying to negotiate a high price for clothing with a buyer at a large store and he or she expresses dissatisfaction with the product that was recently shipped. What would you do to resolve the situation? How would you try to maintain a high price for the product you are currently selling?"

It is important to keep in mind that asking questions about past behavior doesn't mean you can't also ask about hypothetical situations that are predictive about future behavior as well. This is important because asking about past behavior alone when interviewing a candidate with limited experience may lead you to screen him or her out because the candidate hasn't been in that situation. Using situational interview questions (future-oriented) allows you to assess potential even if they haven't experienced that particular situation. *Research has shown asking questions about past behaviors or asking questions about potential behavior in hypothetical situations are both strong predictors of actual performance.* In fact, asking about potential behavior using situational questions is more highly correlated with intelligence than asking about past behavior in actual situations.

One example where both past or current behavior description is focused on while also future capability gets equal attention is in the course of planning for management continuity or succession. In the planning for business continuity, it is vital to assess not only the performance of the individual (today) but also the potential to do bigger, greater things, tomorrow. The rule of thumb in the Fortune 500 is to identify great people and give them larger roles. This means learning people's potential to perform in roles or on matters for which they may not bring relevant past experience.

For instance, in business, individual contributors who managed teams enterprise-wide to solve a problem exhibit the potential to become a manager. In law enforcement, officers thrown into life-threatening situations make command decisions in the moment, demonstrating leadership potential.

The point to remember is that the individual being assessed may not have the specific experience desired for the new role(s) in their past; however, in the course of the interview, you learn that they actually handled situations or challenges that called for characteristics needed in the new assignment—implicating the potential to learn or handle the new assignment. Good interviewers distill elements from the past, present, and future by blending hypothetical scenarios, behavioral descriptions, and situational questions. The result is a powerful biography and better predictions about success and better prescriptions for development.

Finally, the context of future performance is relevant. Under what circumstances or conditions will they be working? Will the individual need to perform in life-threatening situations? Is the person entering a harsh business environment? Is the capital investment compatible with the stakeholder expectations? Is there cultural confusion that requires clarity? What are the consequences of a mistake—product launch delays, operational inefficiencies, innovation suffocation, or on larger, human matters—job loss, bankruptcy, or perhaps lives can be at stake as is the case in law enforcement and private security occupations.

As always, benchmarks or descriptions of bad, good, and even better responses can be crafted in advance of the interview regardless of whether past, present, or future-oriented questions be asked. The interview protocol should benefit from "subject matter experts" or those "in-the-know" to assure that the questions asked are job-related (i.e., valid) and that you sample from critical situations the candidate will need to handle in the future.

12. Action Item

Consider computerized interviewing to get the factual data.

Rationale

Technology has touched the interview. Questions can be delivered via computer in an interactive, conversational manner. The interface can be designed to "feel" like a conversation or be more "report-driven" rather than conversational. Computerized interviews do not require an interviewer.

Interacting in a nonsocial context reduces the exaggeration, self-aggrandizement, or desire to place one's foot forward in the best possible light. Not only does computerized interaction reduce "socially desirable responses" but it also seems to enhance truthfulness when reporting factual historical data. Responses to the computer request for information are blunt, simplified, and concrete. It's a highly effective data-capturing device when the situation does not include a need to sample interpersonal dynamics (avatar-type interview processes are being developed).

However, for positions where interpersonal interaction is important, the context of computer interaction—being cold or impersonal—brings unintended (but not entirely unexpected) side effects. Interviewees for senior-level positions are best *not* handled through computer interaction (alone). Computerized interviewing breeds resentment and perhaps anger in people who expect different treatment, "humane" treatment. It is apparently key to treat interviewees in a manner consistent with their self-beliefs or in a manner appropriate for the position or assignment.

The manner in which you treat interviewees impacts the interviewee's response. There is little give and take when reacting to a computer—the implication is that there is little or no need for dialogue. This can be interpreted as rude and offensive—or impersonal, which, of course, it is.

Computerized interviewing is appropriate for some situations—especially if long-term relations are not important. For senior-level professionals, however, it is advisable to not implement a tool (efficient as it is) that breeds bad feelings from the get go. Alternatively, set up the computerized interaction as an administrative process rather than as an interview. Most of us merely get annoyed at administrivia rather than offended.

13. Action Item

Conduct the interview respectfully to decrease litigation risk.

Rationale

Litigation is triggered by interviews as a result of wrongful practices or perceived wrongful practices. Title VII of Civil Rights Act (1964; 1991) protects individuals from wrongful discrimination in the employment context. That is, it is illegal to take into consideration protected class status (race, religion, gender, ethnic status, and national origin) when making personnel decisions. Any method, practice, or procedure is susceptible to legal scrutiny as is the fairness or access to all benefits and privileges of employment. There are various Equal Employment Opportunity Laws that afford protections against being treated illegally when being assessed or interviewed (these being tools that impact employment status). A sample of protections is offered:

Age Discrimination in Employment Act (1967)
- covers most employers with 20 or more employees;
- prohibits employers from discriminating on the basis of age for individuals 40 years of age or older.

Americans with Disabilities Act (ADA) (1990)
- covers most employers with 15 or more employees;
- specifies that it is illegal to take into consideration an applicant's disability unless that disability negates the possibility of performing an essential function of the job.

The candidate does not have to be disabled; mere perception that a disability exists can trigger legal action.

Civil Rights Act (1964)
- prohibits discrimination on the basis of sex, race, color, religion, and national origin;
- covers most employers with 15 or more employees.

Civil Rights Act (1991)
- an amendment to the Civil Rights Act of 1964, this act expands the list of remedies that employees can receive;
- provides a more detailed description of evidence needed to prove a discrimination claim.

Immigration Reform and Control Act (1986)
- prohibits hiring aliens not authorized to work in the United States;
- prohibits employers from discriminating based on citizenship or national origin;
- covers most employers with at least four employees.

Pregnancy Discrimination Act (1978)
- prohibits discrimination against women based on a pregnancy-related condition;
- covers most employers with 15 or more employees.

Vietnam Era Veterans' Readjustment Assistance Act of 1974 (VEVRAA) (Amended in 2002 by the Jobs for Veterans Act)
- prohibits discrimination against and requires affirmative action for disabled veterans as well as other categories of veterans;
- Any contractor or subcontractor with a contract of $25,000 or more with the federal government.

This book is not legal advice but rather is guidance on how to ask question to comply with the law. There are other "EEO Laws" (Equal Employment Opportunity Laws such as Equal Pay Act, 1967; Genetic Information Nondiscrimination Act, 2008) that incidentally could conceivably be affected by how a manager interviews an employee (e.g., "tell me again why as a woman in this role you think I should pay you more?" please see www.eeoc.gov).

Fundamentally, assessment must be based on job-related requirements (human competencies). These requirements should be documented and evaluated in terms of importance to success on the job and when the competency needs to be displayed (i.e., is it a day one requirement or can it be learned over time without compromising overall job performance).

In addition to the obvious fact that the interview cannot violate law, it is important that interviewers be aware that they must ensure that they do not contribute to the *perception* of wrongdoing. The selection interview is not only a legal event it is an emotional event as well. *Interviewers must learn the difference between the intent and the impact of what they say and do during the assessment.*

There is a relationship between how you "treat" the applicant and their reaction. Managers frequently engage in inappropriate behaviors that are likely to trigger litigation. For example, some managers believe they are being efficient when they use their smart phone to complete some tasks during the interview. The job candidate, however, will feel disrespected. Other managers may make the candidate follow them around so they can deal with issues while they conduct the interview. These are true stories. It is important to give each candidate full attention and conduct the interview in a preplanned location. If you view the applicant as a customer (rather than applicant) then it is clear that components of the interview process must be handled thoughtfully and respectfully.

The perception of unfairness is as important as unfairness itself. Both can trigger litigation.

> Reduce the risk of litigation by planning the treatment of all those being interviewed. Are you being considerate? Is it a kind process? Do you care?
> Is your process cold, impersonal, or rude?
> Do you handle the individual in a manner that conveys respect?
> Are you or is your interview process courteous?
> Do your questions raise eyebrows?
> Can the content of your question be linked to job requirements?

You can reduce the risk of litigation by asking questions that are likely to be perceived as legitimate and reasonable. Increase the perception of fairness by explaining the nature of the questions you are to ask, before you ask them. Show respect. Show concern. Give the person a sense of dignity and autonomy. Candidates interpret your willingness to provide an explanation as a sign of respect and this reduces risk. This is true for any interview situation, be it employment related or not. All professionals reduce risk through the simple practice of human courtesy.

Unusual questions trigger internal warning systems. Unusual questions, whether or not they are fair or useful, can enhance litigation risk because they lack credibility in the eyes of the interviewee. Most research in assessment focuses on the statistical or psychometric properties of assessment. Litigation however is prompted by emotion—feeling wronged, mishandled, disrespected, or manipulated.

In employment situations, using unusual questions is not worth the risk because the information desired can likely be obtained using a different set of questions or the information itself may not bring incremental value at all. Unusual questions can be identified by the fact that the "distance" between question content and job requirements is so indirect that the average or reasonable person will not be able to connect them. This does not mean you should not probe, ask for clarification, or be alert to nonverbal messages that require further investigation.

When assessing an individual for employment, remember this:

The perceived legitimacy of interview questions is as important as the job-related content of the question itself.

Interviews can be constructed to reduce litigation. Personnel decision-making tools (interviews) can be designed and administered with professional and legal standards in mind. The needs and perception of the interviewee are worthy of consideration to reduce risk while optimizing interview efficacy.

14. Action Item

Extract more useful information by bringing in an objective, third-party.

Rationale

Avoid polluting the interview process by allowing vested interests to leak into the design and execution of the interview. Get an external, third-party to avoid internal elements that can erode the value of information received or send the interview in the wrong direction.

"We have our own staff; it costs too much: our people can do the job; an outsider doesn't know us; who would we use; who can we trust?" These are all refrains that seem reasonable enough, except for two significant details—if you *really want to know* and if you truly want *honest answers*, people on the inside are disadvantaged—politically, observationally (can't take an outside view) and for selfish reasons, internal views are distorted. Those with a vested interest in outcomes are least likely to seek information (or acknowledge information) that is incongruent with vested interests.

When a specific outcome of an interface can resolve a pressing issue for the interviewer, the interface is polluted. People tend to seek and find what they *need* to seek and find. If an organization needs someone to fill a vacancy rapidly, then most likely one of the candidates being screened will in fact be a good fit. It is unlikely that the pool of candidates will evaporate leaving the interviewer (and the organization) with a persistent problem. It is much easier to find what you think you need because vested interests kill objectivity. This includes the advocate of the person you are interviewing. Don't rely on a representative of an individual to act as an objective third party.

On the interviewee side, if the individual has something to say that is sensitive, confidential, highly personal, incriminating, or critical of the institution or effort, he or she will be reluctant to tell an insider. Offering such information to an "internal" person can be viewed as disloyal and can possibly "get back to him" or be misconstrued, leading to career suicide. No matter how much you, the insider, promise confidentiality and anonymity, the insider (interviewee) will be hesitant. (Whistleblower laws are examples of a legal remedy for this dynamic.)

Outsiders are removed from vested interests, are free from politics, and protect no careers. This person should possess the following characteristics. He or she must (a) be well-versed in data collection and its impact on morale and behavior, (b) be *perceived* as impartial, (c) bring professional credibility, (d) ask questions in a nonjudgmental way, and (e) be nonbiased in thought and manner.

The largest obstacle to truth lies in the hidden desire to avoid it.

15. Action Item

Know how to evaluate information before you collect it.

Rationale

A wise fisherman ponders the bait, the time of the day, and the resources needed to pull the catch in. Like the wise fisherman, skilled interviewers know what they are after, before they go after it. The catch is possible because the end result is known before the ship leaves port.

Interviewers need to do the same. What information do you need? What qualities of the data you are about to collect are useful and what is useless? Have you imposed criteria or objective definition into the information you are about to access? The interview question will capture certain information—is this information capture aligned with your objective needs? Can you link your question and your evaluation criteria?

Build a protocol or scorecard to help you evaluate the utility of information you collect. Getting this "map" to show the information collected and the inference drawn on its basis is invaluable to decision makers. Build a protocol that is embraced by everyone so it will be used during the evaluation of information process. You might catch something but you don't know what it will be or whether you would (or should) be happy about it.

Typically scorecards are designed with (a) the question, (b) the rationale for asking the question, and (c) sample interpretation or evaluations for a possible set of answers. A structured approach to interview information usage ensures that nothing useful will get through your net. Alternatively, the connecting of inferences drawn based on the information collected is in full view of all decision makers and this can minimize unwanted biases or extraneous information leaking into the analytic process. Finally, you will know that you caught what you set out to catch because that is what your net retains.

Suggested Readings

Action Item 1

Cascio, W. (1995). Whither industrial and organizational psychology in a changing world? *American Psychologist 50*, 928–939.

Flanagan, J. C. (1954). The critical incident technique. *Psychological Bulletin 51*, 327–358.

Landy, F. J., & Vasey, J. (1991). Job Analysis: The composite of subject matter expert samples. *Personnel Psychology 44*, 27–40.

McCormick, E. J. (1979). *Job analysis: Methods and applications*, New York, NY: AMACOM.

Action Item 2

Dipboye, R. (1992). *Selection interviews: Process perspective*. Mason, OH: South-Western.

Ghiselli, E. E. (1966). The validity of the personnel interview. *Personnel Psychology 19*, 389–394.

Wright, O. R. (1969). Summary of research on the selection interview since 1964. *Personnel Psychology 22*, 391–413.

Action Item 3

Hammond, K. R., Hursch, C. J., & Todd, F. J. (1964). Analyzing the components of clinical inference. *Psychological Review 71*, 438–456.

Sackett, P., Burris, L., & Ryan, A. (1989). Coaching and practice effects in personnel selection. In C. Cooper & I. Robertson (Eds.), *International review of industrial and organizational psychology*. New York, NY: Wiley.

Young, D. M., & Beier, E. G. (1977). The role of applicant nonverbal communication in the employment interview. *Journal of Employment Counseling 14*, 154–165.

Action Item 4

Diamante, T. (1993). Unitarian validation of a mathematical problem solving exercise. In F. Landy (Ed.), *Journal of Business & Psychology: Special Edition—The Test Validity Yearbook 7*(4), 383–401.

Dunnette, M. D. (1966). *Personnel selection and placement*. Monterey, CA: Brooks/Cole.

Huffcutt, A. I., Conway, J. M., Roth, Philip, L., & Stone, N. J. (2001). Identification and meta-analytic assessment of psychological constructs measured in employment interviews. *Journal of Applied Psychology 86*(5), 897–913.

Society for Industrial & Organizational Psychology. (1987). *Principles for the validation and use of personnel selection procedures* (3rd ed.), Bowling Green, OH: SIOP Publications.

Action Item 5

Campion, M. A., Palmer, D., & Campion, J. E. (1997). A review of structure in the selection interview. *Personnel Psychology 50*, 655–702.

Dipboye, R. (1992). *Selection interviews: Process perspectives.* Mason, OH: South-Western.

Huffcutt, A. I., & Arthur, W., Jr. (1994). Hunter and Hunter (1984) revisited: Interview validity for entry level jobs, *Journal of Applied Psychology 79*, 184–190.

Van Iddekinge, C. H., Raymark, P. H., & Roth, P. L. (2005). Assessing personality with a structured employment interview: Construct-related validity and susceptibility to response inflation. *Journal of Applied Psychology 90*, 536–545.

Action Item 6

Campion, M., Palmer, D., & Campion, J. (1997). A review of structure in the selection interview. *Personnel Psychology 50*, 655–702.

Gatewood, R., & Feild, H. (2003). *Human Resource Selection.* Fort Worth: Dryden Press.

Action Item 7

Campion, M. A., Palmer, D. K., & Campion, J. E. (1997). A review of structure in the selection interview. *Personnel Psychology 50*, 655–702.

Harris, M. M., & Eder, R. W. (1999). The state of employment interview practice: Commentary and Extension. In R. W. Eder & M. M. Harris (Eds.), *The employment interview handbook.* Thousand Oaks, CA: Sage Publications.

Action Item 8

Goldstein, I., Zedeck, S., & Schneider, B. (1993). An exploration of the job analysis—content validity process. In N. Schmitt, W. Borman & Associates (Eds.), *Personnel selection in organizations* (pp. 3–34). San Francisco, CA: Jossey-Bass.

Williamson, L. G., Campion, J. E., Malos, S. B., Roehing, M. V., & Campion, M. A. (1997). Employment interview on trial: Linking interview structure with litigation outcomes. *Journal of Applied Psychology 82*, 900–912.

Action Item 9

Goldstein, I., & Zedeck, S. (1996). Content validation. In. R. Barrett (Ed.), *Fair employment strategies in human resource management* (pp. 27–46). Westport, CT: Quorum Books.

Seberhagen, L. (1996). A modern approach to minimum qualifications. In. R. Barrett (Ed.), *Fair employment strategies in human resource management* (pp. 164–170). Westport, CT: Quorum Books.

Action Item 10

Huffcutt, A., & Woehr, D. (1999). Further analysis of employment interview validity: A quantitative evaluation of interviewer-related structuring methods. *Journal of Organizational Behavior 20*, 549–560.

Posthuma, R., Morgeson, F., & Campion, M. (2002). Beyond employment interview validity: A comprehensive narrative review of recent research and trends over time. *Personnel Psychology 55*, 1–81.

Pulakos, E., Schmitt, N., Whitney, D., & Smith, M. (1996). Individual differences in interviewer ratings: The impact of standardization, consensus discussion and sampling error on the validity of a structured interview. *Personnel Psychology 49*, 85–102.

Wiesner, W., & Cronshaw, S. (1988). A meta-analytic investigation of the impact of interview format and degree of structure on the validity of the employment interview. *Journal of Occupational Psychology 61*, 275–290.

Williamson, L. G., Campion, J. E., Malos, S. B., Roehing, M. V., & Campion, M. A. (1997). Employment interview on trial: Linking interview structure with litigation outcomes. *Journal of Applied Psychology 82*, 900–912.

Action Item 11

Berry, C. M., Sackett, P. R., & Landers, R. N. (2007). Revisiting interview–cognitive ability relationships: Attending to specific range restriction mechanisms in meta-analysis. *Personnel Psychology 60*(4), 837–874.

Fitzwater, T. L. (2000). *Behavior based interviewing: Selecting the right person for the job.* Menlo Park, CA: Crisp Publications.

Huffcutt, A. I., Roth, P. L., & McDaniel, M. A. (1996). A meta-analytic investigation of cognitive ability in employment interview evaluations: Moderating characteristics and implications for incremental validity. *Journal of Applied Psychology 81*, 459–473.

McDaniel, M., Whetzel, D., Schmidt, F., & Maurer, S. (1994). The validity of employment interviews: A comprehensive review and meta-analysis. *Journal of Applied Psychology 79*, 599–616.

Posthuma, R., Morgeson, F., & Campion, M. (2002). Beyond employment interview validity: A comprehensive narrative review of recent research and trends over time. *Personnel Psychology 55*, 1–81.

Action Item 12

Martin, C. L., & Nagao, D. H. (1989). Some effects of computerized interviewing on job applicant responses. *Journal of Applied Psychology 74*, 72–80.

Roch, S., & Ayman, R. (2005). Group decision making and perceived decision success: The role of communication medium. *Group Dynamics: Theory & Research 9*, 15–31.

Strauss, S. G., & McGrath, J. E. (1994). Does medium matter? The interaction of task type and technology on group performance and member reactions. *Journal of Applied Psychology 79*, 87–97.

Action Item 13

Glynn, C. L., & Marshall, Q. E. (2005). Avoiding a "pounding" in employment litigation: A few ounces of prevention. *The Psychologist-Manager Journal 8*, 121–130.

Rynes, S. L., & Connerly, M. L. (1993). Applicant reactions to alternative selection procedures. *Journal of Business & Psychology Spring*, 261–277.

Steiner, D. D., & Gilliland, S. W. (1996). Fairness reactions to personnel selection techniques in France and the United States. *Journal of Applied Psychology, April*, 124–141.

Uniform Guidelines on Employment Selection Procedures (Washington DC, Bureau of National Affairs, 1979).

Action Item 14

Lowman, R. L. (1998). *The ethical practice of psychology in organizations*. Washington, DC: American Psychological Association.

Maurer, S. (2002). A practitioner-based analysis of interviewer job expertise and scale format as contextual factors in situational interviews. *Personnel Psychology 55*, 307–327.

Schein, E. H. (1967). *Process consultation*. Reading, MA: Addison-Wesley.

Action Item 15

Latham, G. P., & Flanagan, B. J. (1993). Perceived practicality of unstructured, patterned and situational interviews. In H. Schuler, J. L. Farr, & M. Smith (Eds.), *Personnel selection and assessment: Individual and organizational perspectives*. Mahwah, NJ: Erlbaum.

Pearlman, K., & Stoffey, R. W. (1993). Applicant reactions to selection procedures. *Personnel Psychology 46*, 49–76.

SECTION II

Interact, Discover, and Reflect

This section is about the role of the interviewer in affecting the responses of the interviewee. Despite the need to be structured, systematic, and calculated, the interview is not a cold, sterile process. The interview is interplay. In fact, the value of the interview resides in the dialogue that defines the interplay. This section offers advice on how to conduct the interview in order to squeeze as much value out of the interplay as possible. Section I told us how to plan and design the interview to optimize its validity or accuracy. This section focuses not on *what* questions to ask but rather *how* to ask them.

1. Action Item

Past behavior predicts future behavior—breaking this rule of thumb requires compelling information, and coupling questions about the past with questions about the future is a powerful combination (especially when past relevant behavior may not exist).

Rationale

All students of human behavior learn that the best prediction of future behavior is past behavior. Interviews, using situational questions or role-play scenarios, strive to sample past behavior so that accurate predictions about future behavior can be made. "Tell me about a time when ..." or "How would you handle a situation where ..." The stem of each question should include a problem or circumstance that translates into the requirements of a future job or challenge.

To a large extent, the resume is a sampling of past behavior. The interview is also a sampling of stated behavior and exhibited behavior.

Together, inferences are drawn about competencies or capabilities. Undoubtedly, when past behavior suggests deficiencies or incompetence, this evidence-based inference is difficult to challenge. However, a past track coupled with learning and new insights (often a significant life event) might in fact bring new possibilities—negating the behavioral past.

One must also be careful not to use vague generalities about "past behavior" without getting into the details of those behaviors. Behavioral prediction includes the concept of "situational specificity"—that is, while general descriptions may offer some degree of understanding, better prediction is ascertained by knowing how an individual behaves in particular circumstances or situations. An individual might be quite distant from people in general, yet, when he or she is held accountable for others, suddenly behavior is altered and this desire for distance is not noticeable or even recognizable.

Alternatively, an individual might offer a story of transformation such as a story of a person who carries the burden of underachievement yet offers a proposition of change.

For instance, a nondescript candidate reveals that a car fell onto his chest (while tinkering with the engine) and revelation hits him—he has no past worthy of mentioning and his career path is unimpressive as is other aspects of the individual's life. He speaks about what it was like to face death and then overcoming that event and to face choices and possibilities that, for some reason, never seemed possible before the tragedy. He speaks of this with vigor and animation and even wonder. He recovers fully from the life-threatening (or life-creating) injury and enters a top-tier graduate school (at age 32). After 10 years of effort, he runs a business valued at $10M—and he owes it all to a car falling on his chest.

To reiterate, please be careful not to limit questioning to only past behavior. You can (and often must) ask questions about hypothetical situations and future behavior. Also, compelling information about individual change might be present if you probe and remain open to the possibility that it exists. If you don't look for it, you won't find it.

Interviewees will not always bring past behavior that is useful (or may not recall relevant past behavior) and yet they will be terrific job candidates as they articulate what they would do, could do, and want to do in order to handle the situations you verbally pose. They also may lack the specific job-relevant experience but may bring the capability to learn rapidly and, therefore, will be able to handle the job or the challenge. Worth noting is the fact that research tells us that situational interview questions (i.e., "how would you go about handling a complex situation where ...") are better indicators of cognitive ability than behavior description interview questions (i.e., "tell me what you did when ..."). While there are many (and better) ways to measure analytical or cognitive ability, it is worth noting that in gaining a sense of potential or intellectual might, situational interviews that are future-oriented are a good way to go.

2. Action Item

Avoid bias that is wrong, unfair, and possibly illegal by using training, independent evaluations, and crosschecking.

Rationale

Interviews can be improvised to some extent but they require a firm foundation, a method, or a purpose before they begin. Improvisation can make things interesting but—without the coordination or better said, "standardization," there is no music—in fact, it is really just noise. Avoid access to information that may contaminate your perspective before you meet the person. This includes comments from others who will have (but have not yet) met the candidate and, most importantly, stay close to the structure of the interview protocol.

The fundamentals of the interview include planning to ensure that everything is done, that can be done, to optimize fairness or accuracy. To do this, job-related questions comprise the cornerstones of the interview. These questions are prewritten to optimize access to the information desired. This also safeguards the interview from "being pulled" in the direction of assumptions or biases made before the interview even started.

Bias leaks into judgments of interviewers through many sources and as a result of interactions between sources. Interviewers should be aware of the sources of contamination and their role in this interplay. A few biases include diversity-linked differences that lead to wrong, naïve, or misguided inferences about people; the assumption of traits or characteristics based on physical features (physiognomy), and information-processing errors such as rating an individual wonderful in many ways because that person is viewed positively on one characteristic in particular. Other rating errors also come into play such as contrasting the interviewee with others instead of against the purpose of the evaluation or the job requirements themselves.

Training and cross-evaluations minimize bias by bringing various perspectives to the review of the candidate (nonsystematic bias). Educating interviewers about biases that can leak into how questions are asked and how interviewees are judged is critical. It is advised that simulations be used to train interviewers and they should include feedback to the interviewer about how they were perceived by the interviewee (videotaping is worth the effort) and highlight bias when it exists or demonstrate how it was avoided.

Common mistakes to avoid:

- Wrongful discrimination based on protected class status
- Contrast errors (comparing interviewees rather than interviewees against job requirements)
- Halo errors (positive rating on one characteristic extended to all characteristics)
- Gender role bias (assuming job role is suitable for only one gender)
- Similar-to-me error (preferring interviewees that are similar to the interviewer)

Fundamental elements of interviewer training cannot and should not be disregarded. To do so is to assume a level of risk that is unnecessary.

3. Action Item

Overcome communication barriers by aligning your manner of speech with the perspective of the interviewee.

Rationale

Avoid behaviors that hinder communication. Competent communication requires attention to your audience, understanding the psyche of the audience, and adaptive communications capability.

Interviewers must avoid behaviors that hinder effective communication and must learn to identify common communication barriers in order to achieve a successful interview or communicate purposefully.

The first step in an effective interview is to recognize and avoid behaviors that hinder communication, which include:

- Avoid the use of technical jargon
- Do not inject sociocultural biases (even if being done casually)
- Never dismiss a concern
- Avoid reading and writing notes when focused attention is called for
- Do not send signals that can be interpreted as disinterest (or evasiveness)
  - Don't break eye contact when informing
  - Don't look away when you are asked a direct question
  - Don't cross your arms, ever or do it comfortably (and open them intermittently)
  - Don't slouch in your chair
  - Don't overassert verbally or nonverbally (this can seem aggressive)

For instance, interviewers should avoid frequent interruptions when an interviewee is telling his or her own story, and should allow use of nonbiased questions and echo the interviewee's word and affect to express unconditional positive regard toward self-expression.

Some general guidelines to avoid unnecessary obstacles to healthy communication:

1. Explain the purpose and process of the interview immediately.
2. Ask ALL candidates if any accommodations are necessary before the application and interview process begins (refer to American with Disabilities Act, 1990; http://www.eeoc.gov/facts/fs-ada.html).
3. Provide reasonable accommodation before the interview begins; this may include amplification of sound or using an interpreter (sign language), as examples.
4. Keep alert for verbal and nonverbal signs of distress that could be triggered by inability to hear or understand what you are saying (especially in the beginning of the interview).

5. Don't misinterpret a disability to infer overall deficiencies; not only do you violate ADA law (1990) but you also wrongfully underestimate, undervalue, and underutilize the capable person in front of you (e.g., hearing deficiencies do *not* correlate with poor reading comprehension, poor judgment, or inability to learn); additionally, if you assume an applicant has a disability, then even if an applicant doesn't have a disability you can still be subject to a legal challenge of discrimination.
6. Look for an open-ended way to overcome barriers: use open-ended questions without an hidden agenda; avoid being judgmental.
7. Recognize any mental status change during the interview process as these can be used as "signals" (sometimes sent inadvertently) that your communications style is faulty.

Understanding these common communication barriers are core concepts in medical interviews, litigation consulting, and employment interviews. Understanding the dynamics of effective communications involving human emotions, intensity of the questioning, consequences of the process, time pressure, and the stakes involved are all significant elements that need to be weighed to improve the efficacy of questioning and interviewing.

4. Action Item

Minimize individual quirks or biases through training.

Rationale

Interviewers who conduct selection interviews are empowered to make a high-stakes decision about an individual. Personal blind spots may prevent them from integrating important information into this critical decision. Organizational decision makers tend to select and promote people who resemble themselves. Organizations tend to become homogeneous over time as they often attract and retain people who are more similar than dissimilar. As a result, this may threaten their ability to adapt and survive. Therefore, it is important to include diverse views and standardize preparatory training to guard against a tendency to prefer "sameness." The requirements driving the interview, once again, should be derived from a competitive analysis of the business situation and in a related fashion, drilling that analysis down into the actual requirements of the jobs being filled.

Decisions can be improved by including a mix of perspectives into the hiring decision. The decision can be made jointly by a variety of individuals who will ultimately work with the new hire and are cognizant of the business situation or circumstances in which the individual will be working.

For example, in addition to the hiring official/manager or his or her representative, the input from customers, peers, subordinates, or others can be valuable. Each of these stakeholders will interact with the individual in different ways. Multiple sources of input bring new perspectives and added context.

Mixing interviewers means mixing different attributes of interviewers and this is not without its drawbacks. Incorporate a "process focus" on all aspects of the interview when multiple interviewers are involved. Add to the mix with a planned strategy. What perspectives do you want on the interviewee and why? What do the various interviewers bring that is different and useful? Training and preparation on such matters is invaluable in making sure the interview process is "clean"—being focused on job requirements, ensuring standardization of delivery, and in benefiting from relevant perspectives in the interpretation of the information collected. Consider a facilitator to ensure that differing viewpoints have a chance to surface during the decision-making process.

5. Action Item

Separate preinterview impressions from post-interview analysis.

Rationale

What you might think about persons before you meet them can influence how you evaluate them after you meet them. Generally, this is true regardless of how the person behaves when you do meet or interview them. This can be good or bad.

To the extent that the resume or past track record reflects effectiveness in specific environments, it is useful information. If lackluster interview performance is a result of extraneous factors unrelated to the individual's competence *per se*—illness, bad interview questions, preconceived notions, fatigue—then, of course, the preinterview "paper" information can be more important than the interview information. The exception is if, of course, "interview performance" is viewed as a credible, needed skill. Still, one-time assessments are exactly that: one-time assessments that are limited in time, scope, and method.

The problem is that you never really know what causes a bad interview; and to leap to a conclusion that contradicts an impressive paper trail is not immediately wise. In addition, if the purpose of the interview is fact gathering, and not assessment of the individual, it is advantageous and wise to consider that the person's inability to perform might be due to a lack of something other than motivation. Try again to get the information you need under different circumstances, at a different time, and share the need to do this—you may be surprised to find the uncooperative or distanced individual suddenly appreciative, warm, and accepting of your offer.

Best treatment:

- Address your concern before the interview ends.
"I don't mean to get off track but I'm feeling like you are disinterested, distracted, or just not into this interview–is there something you'd like to share?"
"It is difficult to really know a person based on limited time in an interview, but I am concerned that you might not think this job is right for you or generally I am not picking up that this excites you at all—am I misreading you or is there something else going on?"

If behavior does not seem aligned with history (jobs held in high credibility places)—stop the interview. Pause. And say:

"I don't mean to be critical, but I am noticing that you are very fidgety, not really listening to me or being evasive (whatever the case may be)—given your impressive background this doesn't seem to fit for me—is there something on your mind getting in your way of interviewing today? Can I help? I want to get to know you better but you don't seem to be yourself"

Asking open questions, such as these, invites disclosure. The disclosure could lead to learning about a difficult morning for the interviewee (e.g., terrible event at home), the fact that the individual is under severe financial burdens (caused by factors outside of the individual's control) and this is getting in their way of being him or herself, or other matters. The point is there could be issues on the table that are making it impossible for the interviewer to easily see the true capability of the interviewee. Indeed, with a better understanding of circumstances surrounding the interviewee, better judgment can be applied.

Being aloof, distracted, overly wordy, smiling too much, or being overly expressive—all could be useful information to the interviewer. The onus is on the interviewer to utilize all behavior during the interview relative to other known aspects of the person to make sound judgments. Many interviewers will shut down under these circumstances. Big mistake. Instead of shutting down when behavior appears misaligned with other sources of information during the interview, open up! Ascertain what is influencing the person if behavior seems misaligned based on other sources of information about the person or if what you are seeing or hearing is not fitting with other facts about the person.

Consider controlling how information about a person is shared and when, both before and after an interview. Realize that access to information affects the process of gathering information and consequently controls need to be put into place to ensure desired outcomes are realized.

6. Action Item

Set the stage to ensure that responses are influenced by factors you care about and not those you do not care about.

Rationale

Interviewees are judged best when they are placed in situations that reflect the context of actual job or performance situations for which they are being assessed. It is important to set the stage. The interview should also reflect the level of intensity, seriousness, or demand that will be required of the interviewee relative to the job or performance you expect.

It is essential that prior to conducting an interview, the interviewer reviews the job or situation requirements, prepares competency definitions (what human capabilities are being deemed necessary), structures questions to capture competency-relevant information, and establishes objective evaluation standards. The context of the interview should mirror performance expectations.

In preparing the physical environment, the interviewer should ensure that room arrangements are conducive to conducting the interview by locating a quiet, distraction-free environment. Interviewers can help candidates feel comfortable by making introductions, avoiding inappropriate questions, and building rapport by initiating "small talk." Whatever intensity is engineered into the interview, this intensity should be realistic, essential, and not contrived.

Do not be perfunctory—this is the classic interview flaw.

Before proceeding with the interview, the interviewer should also explain the structured nature of the interview, that all candidates will be asked the same questions, that it is acceptable for the candidate to quietly consider responses, that notes will be taken, state the anticipated approximate length of the interview, and indicate there will be an opportunity at the end to ask questions of the interviewer. This is very obvious but often neglected.

It takes some practice, but it is critical that the structured interview questions be read in a natural, conversational tone while detailed notes are taken and eye contact and rapport are maintained. Effective interviewers manage to juggle these activities to yield relevant responses and record behavior relevant to targeted competencies.

7. Action Item

Avoid specific errors by knowing and using an interview methodology that will enable the expression of the information desired.

Rationale

Decisions regarding how information is to be used will drive the format and content of the interview. If many decision makers will view interview results, for instance, more formal, evaluative benchmarks are often created by demand. Generally, when fewer interviewers are involved, the process is more likely to be "loose" where the structure of the interview and decision-making criteria are not standardized. This is not good.

Loose interviews are bad assessment devices. Establish what information is going to be targeted and captured based on what you need to know rather than based on the logistics of the interview situation. If you plan how a decision will be made, you can catch costly errors and fix them *in advance*.

For instance, singular interviewers typically fall victim to impressions made on the basis of weak information or impressions formed that reflect interviewer bias. An objective set of criteria to evaluate the candidate can save the interviewer from relying too heavily on one impression (whether this impression is right or wrong). Ensuring that objective criteria are used to evaluate the collected interview information protects against the bias that can leak into decision making by the individual interviewer.

The "oral board" is widely used to ensure checks and balances among interviewers (to control for unwanted bias) and, when structured, these are highly effective protocols to assess competence. During a typical oral board, the applicant is asked to describe how they would handle a series of job-related situations. The responses are benchmarked against preset preferred (or best) responses based on the judgments of subject-matter experts (people who know the job or competency area). The oral is essentially a situational, behaviorally based, structured interview with multiple observers (evaluators), all of whom measure the responses using the same yardstick. (Single interviewer and panels or oral boards can both be valid. The panel involves many and so is a useful way to gain organizational momentum for the candidate.)

Generally, these interview questions are highly structured. The oral boards are conducted by thoroughly trained panels of interviewers, who themselves might be senior job incumbents. Key concerns during the oral board process include comprehensive interviewer training, standardized administration, and maintaining security of interview-related materials. The fact that a "board" is asking, discussing, and jointly evaluating brings special focus to:

- facilitating evaluative discussions
- consensus or decision by vote decision making
- standardizing language to assuage different interpretations
- coordinating question asking
- managing the process of probing the interviewee

How interviews are conducted impacts the requirements for preparing to conduct them to optimize data collection and accuracy. Do not short-change the need to coordinate the asking of questions. Process is as important to an effective interview as are the questions themselves.

8. Action Item

Use nonverbal cues to test your inferences.

Rationale

Nonverbal cues can be indicators of internal emotional states and bring needed context to verbal statements. These are useful only to the extent that the interviewer incorporates them into a valid interview question. The reason for this is that interviewers are not very good at "reading" such cues and thus it can be prone to bias—therefore, it is fine to have your intuitive radar on "high" but validate what you are thinking by verifying through follow-up questions. In interview parlance, this is often called the floating of "trial balloons."

Some examples:

> "You seem uncomfortable with the idea of confronting customers that are very upset, please tell me more about how you would handle an irate customer."

"I get the sense that being accountable for financials for this organization is not something you want to own, can you please tell me what your thinking is in that regard?"

"I don't think you are all that interested in being in a role that has administrative requirements."

The point is that "cues" might be cues and useful toward asking a follow-up, confirmatory, job-related question or these "cues" might be "miscues"—so don't rely on them in and of themselves. Use them only as a suggestion or trial balloon—to ascertain more specifically and behaviorally what the person is thinking or how they are reacting to your question. Again, as humans, we are not good at reading emotional cues, and as interviewers, we certainly should not draw inferences based on them.

Interview data can be broken down into nonverbal and verbal. It is estimated that 60–65% of meaning in a social encounter (such as an interview) is driven by nonverbal communication. Nonverbal (automatic) cues are found to be less susceptible to censorship than verbal communication although training can alter that fact. Freud informed us that "emotions ooze from every pore" when we communicate. The onus is therefore on the interviewer to identify and utilize nonverbal information in an effective manner. Importantly, in practice, interviewers are not good at drawing inferences that are valid based on non-behavioral evidence. In short, interviewers must guard against "fooling themselves" to think they know what a body movement means or they can interpret the underlying meaning of an expression that is almost imperceptible.

Forms of nonverbal communication include paralanguage (speech disturbance), physical appearance (cosmetic features such as make-up, clothes), facial expression (gaze, grimace, muscular changes in the face), kinesis (identifiable body movements), and proxemics (interpersonal distance relationship). Nonverbal reactions are often related to verbal communications. People tend to act in a manner consistent with their speech.

Some researchers argue that nonverbal cues are a primary method of expressing emotion. Nonverbal cues can uncover the interviewee's attempt to hide emotional importance of issues that cannot be expressed overtly. The good interviewer verifies thoughts or concerns that are built based on emotional or subjective or even an intuitive radar. This process of verification separates the amateur from the professional interviewer.

If you ask "The job will require that you travel 80% of the time—will this be a burden for you?" and the candidate states that it is not a problem but can't maintain eye contact and quickly looks away, what do you conclude? Perhaps burdened by the need to obtain the job (financial pressures) the individual, at an emotional level, sends a distress signal—with the emotion overriding the intellect (perhaps to the candidate's disadvantage). This requires follow-up and verification by the interviewer, but it is key that the subtle gesture is noticed—and then acted upon in the form of objective verification.

The importance of nonverbal cues lies in congruency (or lack thereof) with verbal messages. For the interviewer, the question is how to best use these signals as an interviewing tool. Nonverbal messages are smoke signals begging for clarification, probing, and confirmation. Congruence between verbal and nonverbal communication is sometimes clean and obvious. For example, when a patient complains of severe abdominal pain (verbal cue) and this is accompanied by a painful facial expression (nonverbal cue), or when someone has a severe chest pain (verbal cue) accompanied by a clenched fist over the lower sternum (nonverbal cues). In the employment context, search for the entire message and not just the singular path of communication (i.e., the words spoken). For instance, a job candidate verbalizes interest in a sales position for a controversial product while simultaneously signaling distaste through facial expression.

Nonverbal cues assist in confirming hypotheses, leading to an accurate assessment of conditions during the interview according to research. The tough part of this is the practice.

The science of facial expressions is formative and specialized by professionals working in fields such as litigation consulting, investigative interviewing, and in research arenas such on human emotion and expression (e.g., Paul Ekman). Interviewers optimize nonverbal cues by probing, testing, or clarifying to make certain that the inference you are generating based on the nonverbal or the lack of congruity between the nonverbal and the verbal is, in fact, meaningful. *Do not rest any conclusion on a nonverbal cue unless you have confirmatory objective evidence for doing so.* Interviewers are very poor at lie detection in practice. If someone tells you otherwise, it's a lie.

9. Action Item

Communicate accountability to interviewers to improve efficacy.

Rationale

Interviewers who are accountable and know their accountability make better decisions than interviewers who are not accountable or do not realize their accountability. Certainly, those who are attentive to the work they do are preferential to those who are inattentive. Informing interviewers that they will be required to justify their decisions to others enhances the caliber of the interview. Up the pressure by also telling them that they will need to show behavioral evidence to support their inferences.

Apparently, the knowledge of being accountable activates the attention or diligence to the task. Interviewers think longer and harder when they understand their accountabilities. Interviewers process information in a less-biased manner and generally make more accurate decisions when they need to justify their conclusions. In addition, search activity increases (more probing and testing of understanding) during the interview process when there is pressure to connect conclusions to information collected.

Inform interviewers about their role and

- monitor the interviewers
- inform them that others will be overlooking the process
- require that judgments be justified
- evaluate the accuracy of the information-gathering process

While looking over the interviewer's shoulder can inhibit performance, informing interviewers about an inherent process that is being used and their role in that process can improve the value of the interview.

10. Action Item

Establish a given length of time for the interview.

Rationale

Affording a specific amount of time to the interview decreases biases that often leak into judgment and decision making. The longer the time set, the less likely that silly, naïve, immature assessments will impose themselves on the evaluation. Getting to know someone takes time.

When interviews are left to the discretion of the interviewer, the risk of personal bias and immature decision-making processes is increased.

Specifically, by allowing at least sixty minutes (60 minutes) the interviewer is less likely to:

- form and make decisions based on first impressions
- attend to superficial facts, data, or observations
- ask cosmetic or perfunctory questions
- be influenced too heavily by negative information
- make accept/reject decisions within the first few minutes of the interview

It is typical that bias arrives early in the interview and remains. This bias influences what questions are asked, when they are asked, and of course their direction. Immediately "liked" candidates are tagged and follow-up questions "justify" the early decision. Disliked candidates experience a different set of follow-up questions. In neither situation are the candidates truly assessed. Interestingly, the interviewer often feels "confident" in their judgments because the information collected "matches" their intuitive or first impression. This is a rather circular, ineffective assessment process. It is also ubiquitous in the arena of interviewing. By simply requiring interviewers to spend an hour with each person, bias is reduced and decisions enhanced.

11. Action Item

Know essential requirements of the job so that you can adhere to standards set by disability laws.

Rationale

It is estimated that between the fall of 1997 and the fall of 2011, over 270,000 charges were filed with the Equal Employment Opportunity Commission (EEOC) by employees in the private sector under the ADA law. (see http://www.eeoc.gov/eeoc/statistics/enforcement/ada-charges .cfm for the specific statistics.) The EEOC is the federal agency responsible for the enforcement of laws protecting employees from wrongful discrimination. The key to compliance is knowledge about essential job features. The lack of this knowledge exposes the interviewer to risk by asking questions that are not readily linked to "essential" (and not merely useful) aspects of the job.

Under the ADA, disability discrimination occurs when an employer treats a qualified individual with a disability who is an employee or applicant unfavorably because she or he has or may have a disability (see http://www.eeoc.gov/laws/types/disability.cfm) or is perceived to possess a disability ("being regarded to have a disability"). The ADA protects disabled individuals (or individuals perceived as being disabled) from being discriminated against in the selection process by being eliminated from the applicant pool on the assumption that they cannot perform a job requirement or meet expectations of the employer. When this requirement or job demand is not deemed essential and is used as a rejection factor, discrimination is taking place. However, when the rejection is based on failure to perform an essential job feature and it would be unreasonable for the employer to alter or accommodate the disability so that it no longer impacts performance then the disability can be used as a reason for rejection.

Interviewers misunderstand ADA and often fail to learn the requirements of the job or stipulate the mission, goals, and objectives of the position. This flaw places risk on the interviewer, the employer, and most importantly the applicant who might be rejected wrongfully and illegally.

Simple errors such as asking an individual whether they can perform the essential functions of a job *with* accommodation instead of asking an individual whether they can perform the essential functions of a job *with or without* accommodation can result in legal challenges under the ADA. Qualified individuals with disabilities are identifiable and employable when the interviewer understands the position requirements and ADA regulations.

Consider, during the interview, that you are identifying the abilities of the person, every individual brings skills and abilities that are mixed. No one is great at everything. Is your candidate offering the skills and abilities you need to do the essential functions of the job?

12. Action Item

Focus on behavior to reduce the impact of common interviewer errors.

Rationale

Measurement is enhanced significantly in the interview by asking questions that are designed to elicit behavioral responses. Theoretical questions such as "What is your idea of a team player?" or "Where do you want to be in 5 years?" tend to generate vague statements or textbook replies. These responses are difficult to evaluate and often require the interviewer to make assumptions that may be unintentionally influenced by biases or irrelevant factors. At a minimum, these sorts of questions generally result in inconsistent interpretations across interviewees and therefore comparative analysis becomes difficult if not impossible. This is not to say that probing or general questions are not useful at all, they can be and these are thoroughly addressed in Section III. For now, please note that general questions can be the lead into an interview but still the interviewer must dig into responses to get at behavioral specifics. It is always important to connect words or descriptions used by a person to behavioral realities (i.e., what they did and how they did it).

To minimize interviewer error and biases, interview questions should be specifically framed to elicit behavioral evidence of an individual's standing on a specific characteristic worth measuring. Responses that are behavioral in nature are more specific and verifiable, and they can be more reliably evaluated than vague or future-oriented statements (e.g., "I am an excellent problem solver," "I am a good leader").

Furthermore, deploy a set of lead and probe questions for each dimension or characteristic targeted. Lead questions should be designed to evoke open-ended responses that permit the interviewee to easily draw upon past experiences (e.g., "Describe a situation in which you had to …."). Probe questions seek clarification or additional information about the interviewee's response to the lead question. "Tell me more about …," "Exactly what was the circumstance you were under at the time …?" "What was your rationale for making that decision …?"

While there are a number of variations for structuring interview questions, the most effective paradigm is one that requires interviewees to describe the situation involved, the actions they took, and the result of those actions. It is also significant to uncover the context in which the behavior was elicited. Was there time pressure? Were deadlines unrealistic? What were the consequences of making a judgmental mistake? What exactly was on the line?

If an interviewee fails to provide a full account of performance based on the lead question, predefined probe questions can be relied upon to gain a more complete description. This approach focuses on the specific performance relevant to the targeted dimension or characteristic and leads to consistent, accurate evaluation of interview responses across interviewees.

13. Action Item

Ask the interviewee to state the rationale behind actions or desires.

Rationale

Whether you are seeking a person's employment qualifications, potential fit to succeed in a new venture, or readiness for a new position, it is important to get to the "why" behind the person's actions, thought processes, or stated need.

Understanding rationale that drives interest or seeks opportunity is key. One way to do this is to track decisions made over the span of a career (or life) where you explore the circumstances, the factors that were weighed, and the final decision (or choice) that was made. This past event inventory of decision making brings insight on the key drivers behind the individual and often the dialogue sparks insight in the moment.

The same is true when interviewing a potential client who reveals they have a need for your product or service—"asking the why" behind their need might result in a better product solution or it can lead to uncovering additional needs. It might also suggest ways to sell add-on services or enhance your product.

Often interviewers are satisfied with simple answers even to complex or difficult questions. This may lead to inaccurate inferences or wrong conclusions about the person. While capturing the behaviors of the person, the interviewer can also probe to uncover the motivation behind the actions. Asking "the why" question is a very simple and very powerful way to make it rain.

14. Action Item

Guard against the "similar to me" effect.

Rationale

We like people who are "like" ourselves. Interviewers who are similar to the interviewee in terms of demographics, attitudes, interests, or personality characteristics (e.g., conscientiousness) are likely to inflate their ratings of the interviewee. Measuring the similarity of the interviewer to the interviewee, however, is rarely a goal. The similar-to-me effect is well known in research literature and it is important to note that this effect is not conscious or purposeful. It is an error. It leaks into the assessment unknowingly.

Being similar to the interviewer is not always an advantage. For instance, interviewers who are low in conscientiousness or are not very affable or agreeable may view similar characteristics in others as a plus, rather than a minus. Obviously, such misjudgment happening under the radar can lead to bad placement decisions, inaccurate descriptions of character, and poor results when the person evaluated fails despite such favorable reviews from the interview process.

Avoid this error by following Action Items on structuring interviews and establishing evaluative criteria. The key is to be objective or behavioral in defining what you want to measure and how you will evaluate it. The protocol for evaluating good/bad responses can help the interviewer remain aware of personal biases and avoid their leakage into the assessment of others.

Training of interviewers on the errors we make when evaluating other people is crucial to accurate assessment. This training should include assessment to enhance self-awareness so that personal preferences do not bleed into the judgmental process.

Consider this:

- Do I like the candidate? Why?
- Is my judgment being influenced by non-job-related factors? Are these reasonable? Are they relevant? Are they legal?
- Can I connect the reasons I like this candidate to job requirements (that are present in the job analysis that backs up the requirements identified)?
- Is my thinking being influenced by other interviewer opinions, other interviewee comparisons, or other extraneous factors?

15. Action Item

Ask questions in a style congruent with the content or purpose of the interview.

Rationale

An interviewee wanting to respond correctly to the interviewer will "fall into step" based on the style, manner, and seriousness of the interviewer. When interviewing, keep in mind that perceptive individuals will observe you and relate in a manner based on how you are setting the stage.

As the interviewer, you create the playing field. It is your game. Know your metrics. Make sure you understand the criteria you are using to assess interviewees. Do not behave in a manner that is inconsistent with or incongruent with what you seek to sample. That is, if you are trying to determine if the interviewee has any emotional depth, then it would be ineffective to speak in a light-hearted, fun fashion. The perceptive interviewee will not "get heavy" when you are sending signals about being light. You are the lead, don't mislead.

While you do not want to tell the interviewee how to behave, you certainly do not want to act in a manner that is confusing, inconsistent, or incongruous to the competency you hope to observe. You do not want to (unintentionally) stop the interviewee from expressing qualities that you are interested in seeing. This is a key consideration when deciding how to ask questions (e.g., technology can work for or against you depending on interview purpose). How questions are asked matters.

Interviewers who want to learn about an individual's motivation need to be disclosing, open, and inquisitive. Asking for personal information in a perfunctory manner does not produce thoughtful, self-disclosing information. This can lead to wrongly inferring the lack of a characteristic or a deficiency.

Clearly, if you want emotional depth, ask questions that require thought, personal disclosure, or self-insight. And ask these questions by offering a level of depth and even personal disclosure of yourself. For example, the question, "Over my lifetime I've had to make many choices. It's been difficult. Family considerations, my kids, and of course my desire to challenge myself in my profession. So, tell me how does all that measure up for you? What sacrifices will you need to make to assume this assignment overseas and what are your thoughts about them?"

Set the stage for the interaction you want. Preface your question by sharing a personal story of depth and disclosure. Then, pose the question. The interviewer's behavior establishes the expectation and legitimacy to share at an emotional level.

Align the nature of questions and nature of delivering questions. Don't begin an interview being very jovial and light-hearted then switch gears to intensely business serious without a segue to send the signal that it is time to get down to business.

Clearly, asking questions without intensity or focus then measuring the interviewee against some desired level of intensity or focus is unproductive, wrong, and misguided. Don't play sleight of hand with interview questions. Let interviewees speak for themselves.

16. Action Item

Assess core success characteristics that were identified by your job analysis.

Rationale

It is a challenge to find any business, governmental, or nonprofit entity that does not understand the word "change." Change is the only constant. This reality is understood either because organizations got ahead of the curve or were hit by a curve—change is the immortal constant.

Assessment specialists, often with an eye toward EEOC and other professional resources, focus on the need to "boil down" human characteristics required to perform a job into behavioral terms. Strategically, that makes sense and from a legal standpoint it enables documentation of job-related processes aiding validation or otherwise avoiding wrongful discrimination lawsuits. This is good. However, the constant state of change makes it quite difficult to "solidify" job requirements. Job requirements are fluid elements.

The fluidity of organizational roles makes it increasingly difficult to identify job-specific requirements. Instead, go after characteristics that can be applied in many situations or circumstances making them transportable and therefore more durable (and valuable). When these core competencies are job-related, objective, and standardized into the structure of the interview protocol, then the utility of the interview is increased. You are capturing what you need to predict success on the job—the core, critical, constant knowledge/skills requisite for success.

Here are some examples of characteristics that might turn up to be relevant when you analyze the requirements of jobs.

Learning from mistakes
- views failure as an opportunity to learn
- analyzes errors for the sake of improvement
- maintains optimism in the face of experienced failure

Continuous Learning Orientation
- is motivated to stretch personal capability
- pursues formal and informal learning opportunities
- enjoys interdisciplinary learning
- values knowledge, curious

Resilience
- views challenges as opportunities
- actively engages in healthful mental and physical activities
- demonstrates hardiness and perseverance, especially under difficult circumstances
- overcomes performance challenges regardless of obstacles

Expansiveness
- enjoys leveraging knowledge in a practical fashion
- connects esoteric information to applications that are practical
- links information from different sources to concoct something different
- open to new experiences

Aptitude
- faced learning challenges in formal and informal settings
- presents a record of achievement requiring intellectual strength
- attacks challenges requiring new learning
- willing to learn by developing new insights

The foregoing are characteristics or competencies that play well in organizations that are faced with the need to adapt, so as always, when you analyze the job to identify what it takes to be successful, think broadly and all inclusively. It's perfectly fine to factor into job requirements the need to adapt, innovate, and otherwise improve products, processes, or overall business models.

17. Action Item

Analyze personal beliefs, feelings, and biases so they don't creep into your judgments.

Rationale

Self-awareness is a powerful tool. Knowing yourself brings self-control, improves interpersonal skills, and brings self-direction. As an interviewer, self-awareness enables you to factor yourself into how you are seeing, judging, hearing, and, overall, responding to the candidate.

Sources of personal bias are many and they vary from person to person. Culture, past learning, and social dynamics help explain why biases are present but do little to negate them. Being aware of biases is the first step in removing their impact on judgment.

That said, an applicant for a very challenging international assignment interviewed adequately … but barely interviews adequately. The obstacle, in the interviewer's mind, was a lack of energy or enthusiasm or … there just seemed to be something missing. The assignment had inherent dangers and high risks—this was a critical hire. On reflection, the interviewer realized that the candidate's "accent" must have been giving him this wrong feeling—the speech was slow, rhythmic, and pronunciations were very hard to decipher. "It must be the contrast with my style that is making me think negatively about this guy," thought the interviewer. The interviewer worked hard to understand the candidate, making sure the speech difference did not affect judgment.

The interview was (nearly) over. All that was left was to smile and inform the candidate about next steps as he was on his way overseas to perform life-threatening and life-saving duties. Yet, the interviewer just looked and looked at the candidate in silence instead of closing the interview. Unexpectedly, the interviewer (despite a good interview) lowered a statement directly at the candidate. "You don't want this job, do you?"

With that, the candidate exhibited a ton of emotion, the interview took a new tone—and a bad hire was avoided.

Be careful about your personal biases—but don't assume they are always playing.

18. Action Item

Ask future-oriented, situational questions in addition to probing past events.

Rationale

In addition to asking questions about past events or situations, "tell me about a time when you had to handle a difficult employee," it is also useful to ask about future or hypothetical circumstances. "What would you do if you were faced with a complaint about a personal friend who is also an authority figure at work and the nature of the allegation is very large, perhaps a violation of law?" Situational interview questions focused on the future should be structured and behavioral, just like the past-event approach. To that end, always strive to gain access to behavior.

To do this:

- define exactly the situation or circumstance that was challenging
- state what the person had to do in order to be successful
- articulate with behavioral specificity how the person reacted or would react to a specific situation or incident (this description should begin with an action word—led, created, planned, wrote—all these provide a picture of action)
- get the context right (deadlines, consequences of error, risks involved)
- identify the outcome or result of the actions taken by the person (impact on business, impact on people, impact on the profession, impact on a person)
- ask future-oriented questions that are job specific and lend themselves to collecting behaviorally specific responses (i.e., what would be done, how, and why)

Questions that draw from behavioral responses can demand new interview skills. Behavioral conversations can seem dry and detailed, be this past-event based or future-oriented, and therefore some individuals may purposefully avoid giving details, when in fact that is what the interviewer wants. The onus is on the interviewer to use the tool of the structured interview to draw out the behavioral response, especially when the interviewee is answering the question in general, but providing what is needed specifically.

For instance:

Question: "Tell me about a time or situation where you managed to get a project back on-track and under-budget."
Answer: "I was fortunate to have a really talented team working for me."
Follow-up: "That's great, tell me exactly how did you work with your team to get them to do things you needed them to do?"
Answer "Well, to start, we created a set of action items together that clarified our goals and timelines, then we broke our goals into specific objectives and matched talent to outcomes desired. Once I had consensus on all this …"

Situational interviews resonate with many interviewers because it makes sense to ask someone how they would handle problems or circumstances that you want them to handle in the future. However, keep in mind that these only work when the interview is structured and objective (or behavioral) in focus. Remember that structuring the interview around situations or past events will still require intelligent probing—interviewees may not naturally offer you the objective information you must access.

If you don't get the information you need after you ask the question once, go ahead and ask that question again! Do not keep it a secret that you are asking for the specifics.

While any interview that is structured (and behavioral) will outperform the unstructured approach, the situational interview in particular is appealing because it can be future-oriented or past-focused in fact, the same interview can incorporate both past-oriented and future-oriented job-relevant questions.

Suggested Readings

Action Item 1

London, M., Smither, J., & Diamante, T. (2007). Best practices in leadership assessment. In J. Conger & R. E. Riggio (Eds.), *The Practice of leadership: Developing the next generation of leaders.* San Francisco, CA: Jossey-Bass.

McClelland, D. C. (1973). Testing for competence rather than intelligence. *American Psychologist 28*, 1–14.

Ouellett, J. A., & Wood, W. (1998). Habit and intention in everyday life: The multiple processes by which past behavior predicts future behavior. *Psychological Bulletin 124*, 54–74.

Stogdill, R. M. (1948). Personal factors associated with leadership: A survey of the literature. *Journal of Psychology 25*, 35–71.

Action Item 2

Allport, G. W. (1954). *The nature of prejudice.* Reading, MA: Addison-Wesley.

Cooper, W. H. (1981). Ubiquitous halo. *Psychological Bulletin 90*, 218–244.

Quinn, K. A., & Macrae, C. N. (2005). Categorizing others: The dynamics of person construal. *Journal of Personality and Social Psychology 88*, 467–479.

Schmidt, F. L., & Zimmerman, R. D. (2004). A counterintuitive hypothesis about employment interview validity and some supporting evidence. *Journal of Applied Psychology 89*, 553–561.

Yamauchi, T. (2005). Labeling bias and categorical induction: Generative aspects of category information. *Journal of Experimental Psychology 31*, 538–553.

Action Item 3

Levinson, W. (1993). The effect of two continuing medical education programs on communication skills of practicing physicians. *Journal of General Internal Medicine 8*, 318–324.

Roter, D. L. (1995). Improving physicians' interviewing skills and reducing patients emotional distress. A randomized clinical trial. *Archives of Internal Medicine 95*, 1877–1884.

Action Item 4

Arvey, R. D., & Campion, J. E. (1982). The employment interview: A summary and review of recent research. *Personnel Psychology 35*, 281–322.

Maurer, T. J., Solamon, J. M., Andrews, K. D., & Troxtel, D. D. (2001). Interviewee coaching, preparation strategies and response strategies in relation to performance in situational employment interviews. *Journal of Applied Psychology 86*, 709–717.

Schneider, B., Goldstein, H. W., & Smith, D. B. (1995). The ASA framework: An update. *Personnel Psychology 48*, 747–774.

Sessa, V. I., & Taylor, J. J. (2000). Choosing leaders: More cooks make a better broth. *Consulting Psychology Journal: Practice and Research 52*, 218–225.

Action Item 5

Borman, W. C. (1977). Consistency in rating accuracy and rating errors in the judgment of human performance. *Organizational Behavior and Human Performance 20*, 238–252.

Wherry, R. J., & Bartlett, C. J. (1982). The control of bias in ratings. *Personnel Psychology 35*, 521–551.

Action Item 6

Burnett, J., Fan, C., Motowidlo, S., & Degroot, T. (1998). Interview notes and validity. *Personnel Psychology 51*, 375–396.

Gatewood, R., & Field, H. (2003). *Human resource selection.* Fort Worth: Dryden Press.

Action Item 7

Eder, R. W., & Harris M. M. (Eds.) (1999). *The employment interview handbook.* Thousand Oaks, CA: Sage Publications, Inc.

Latham, G. P., & Finnegan, B. J. (1993). Perceived practicality of unstructured, patterned, and situational interviews. In H. Schuler, J. L. Farr, & M. Smith (Eds.), *Personnel selection and assessment: Individual and organizational perspectives*. Hillsdale, NJ: Lawrence Erlbaum Associates.

Williamson, L. G., Campion, J. E., Malos, S. B., Roehing, M. V., & Campion, M. A. (1997). Employment interview on trial: Linking interview structure with litigation outcomes. *Journal of Applied Psychology 82*, 900–912.

Action Item 8

Ekman, P. (2007). *Emotions revealed: Recognizing faces and feelings to improve communication and emotional life*. New York, NY: Henry Holt & Company.

Nardone, D. A. (1990). Collecting and analyzing data: Doing and thinking. In H. K. Walker, W. D. Hall & J. W. Hurst (Eds.), *Clinical methods*, (3rd edn.) Boston, MA: Butterworth Publ. pp. 22–28.

Stoeckle, J. D., & Billings, J. A. (1987). A history of note-taking in the medical interview. *Journal of General Internal Medicine 2*, 119–127.

Action Item 9

Balzer, W. K., Doherty, M. E., & O'Connor, R. J. (1989). Effects of cognitive feedback on performance. *Organizational Behavior and Human Decision Processes 52*, 292–306.

Brtek, M. D., & Motowidlo, S. J. (2002). Effects of procedure and outcome accountability on interview validity. *Journal of Applied Psychology 87*, 185–191.

Eder, R. W. (1999). Contextual effects. In R. W. Eder & M. M. Harris (Eds.), *The employment interview handbook*. Thousand Oaks, CA: Sage.

Action Item 10

Dipboye, R. L. (1982). Self-fulfilling prophecies in the selection-recruitment interview. *Academy of Management Review 7*, 579–586.

Peters, L. H., & Terborg, J. R. (1975). The effects of temporal placement of unfavorable information and of attitude similarity on personnel decisions. *Organizational Behavior and Human Performance 13*, 279–293.

Webster, E. C. (1982). *The employment interview: A social judgments process.* Ontario: S.I.P. Publications.

Action Item 11

Americans with Disabilities Act of 1990, 42 U.S.C.A.

Colker, R. (1999). Americans with Disabilities Act: A windfall for defendants. *Harvard Civil Rights—Civil Liberties Law Review 34*, 99–162.

Goodman-Delahunty, J. (2000). Psychological impairment under the Americans with Disabilities Act: Legal Action Items. *Professional Psychology: Research & Practice 31*, 197–205.

Action Item 12

Campion, M., Palmer, D., & Campion, J. (1997). A review of structure in the selection interview. *Personnel Psychology 50*, 655–702.

Ellis, A. P. J., West, B. J., Ryan, A. M., & DeShon, R. P. (2002). The use of impression management tactics in structured interviews: A function of question type? *Journal of Applied Psychology 87*, 1200–1208.

Knicki, A. J., Hom, P. W., Trost, M. R., & Wade, K. J. (1995). Effects of category prototypes on performance rating accuracy. *Journal of Applied Psychology 80*, 354–370.

Sears, G., & Rowe, P. (2003). A personality based similar to me effect in the employment interview: Conscientiousness, affect versus competence mediated interpretations and the role of job relevance. *Canadian Journal of Behavioural Science 35*, 13–24.

Zeldeck, S., & Cascio, W. (1984). Psychological issues in personnel decisions. *Annual Review of Psychology 35*, 461–518.

Action Item 13

Del Gaizo, E. R., Lunsford, S., & Marone, M. (2004). *Secrets of top performing salespeople*. New York, NY: McGraw Hill.

Hale, J. (2004). *Performance-based management*. San Francisco: John Wiley & Sons.

Action Item 14

Employment Law Letter. (2004). Lee Smith Publishers & Printer, Washington, DC. May, Volume 4, Issue 12.

Kassin, S. (2005). On the psychology of confessions: Does innocence put innocents at risk? *American Psychologist, 60*, 215–228.

Action Item 15

Sears, G. J., & Rowe, P. M. (2003). A personality-based similar-to-me effect in the employment interview: Conscientiousness, affect-versus competence-mediated interpretations, and the role of job relevance. *Canadian Journal of Behavioural Science 35,* 13–24.

Action Item 16

Kiker, D. S., & Motowidlo, S. J. (1998). Effects of rating strategy on inter-dimensional variance, reliability and validity of interview ratings. *Journal of Applied Psychology 83,* 763–768.

VanDenboss, G. R., & Williams, S. (2000). The internet versus the telephone: What is telehealth, anyway? *Professional Psychology: Research & Practice 31,* 490–492.

Action Item 17

Breakwell, G. M. (1990). Interviewing: Problems in practice series. *British Psychological Society.* Leicester, UK: Blackwell Publishing.

Messmer, M. (2004). Top 10 questions to ask during a job interview. *Strategic Finance. Montvale 86,* 11.

Action Item 18

Campion, M. A., Campion, J. E., & Hudson, J. P. Jr. (1994). Structured interviewing: A note on incremental validity and alternative question types. *Journal of Applied Psychology 79*, 998–1002.

Delargy, K., & Leteney, F. (2005). Managing competencies during times of change. *Knowledge Management Review. Chicago 8*(1), 12.

McDaniel, M. A., Whetzel, D. L., Schmidt, F. L., & Maurer, S. D. (1994). The validity of the employment interviews: A comprehensive review and meta-analysis. *Journal of Applied Psychology 79*, 599–616.

Pulakos, E. D., & Schmidtt, N. (1995). Experience-based and situational interview questions: Studies of validity. *Personnel Psychology 48*, 289–308.

Wiesner, W. H., & Cronshaw, S. (1998). A meta-analytic investigation of the impact of interview format and degree of structure on the validity of the employment interview. *Journal of Applied Psychology 61*, 275–290.

SECTION III

Uncover, Reveal, and Authenticate

The purpose of this section is to offer guidelines useful for interviewing in general. Whereas there are strict legal and professional standards navigating what you can and cannot do during the employment interview, there is also a wealth of research (and practical wisdom) that is useful for anyone relying on the interview to collect information. This section captures the advice of a multidisciplinary team of professionals who rely on the interview to do their job, be this in the employment interview context or not.

1. Action Item

Always explain who you are, the purpose of the interview or assessment, and where the information is going.

Rationale

The circumstance of answering a list of questions is generally stressful for individuals. The set-up of an interviewer with questions and an interviewee who must respond establishes an unequal balance of power that inherently places the interviewee at a disadvantage. Individuals often attempt to gauge external factors, such as prior knowledge about the purpose of the interview, their perception of the interviewer, and their evaluation of the setting to gauge their responses to interviews, including their tone, degree of disclosure, and honesty.

Providing information that reveals important contextual factors about the interview process before you begin the actual questioning establishes rapport, and when this is done in a responsible and positive manner, it can increase the likelihood of honesty and full disclosure during the interview. In addition, it addresses ethical considerations such as informed consent, right to privacy, and protection from harm.

It is good policy to address contextual issues directly at the beginning of the interview. Doing so provides some background to the interviewee, and lays the groundwork from which the interviewee can make decisions about how to respond to the interview. In addition, it sets a tone that the interview is a collaborative endeavor, not a situation in which the interviewer seeks to maintain power thereby bridging the interviewer and the interviewee.

Information to provide at the beginning of the interview includes (a) the interviewer's name and position, (b) the purpose of the interview, (c) where is the information that the interviewee provides going and what it will be used for, (d) general logistical information such as how long the interview will last, location of restrooms, opportunities for breaks, and so forth, and (e) whom to contact in case of questions (this can be the interviewer, a supervisor, or someone else).

2. Action Item

Build rapport rapidly by demonstrating empathy, supporting self-efficacy (confidence), and enhancing a mutual understanding.

Rationale

The inability to build rapport during an interview is never a good thing. Certainly, the fault can be on the candidate—but like all aspects of the interview—rapport is an outcome of interactions and so the competent interviewer needs to make sure key ingredients are present. While there is no silver bullet, research is starting to identify core ingredients that appear to be present in healthy, interpersonal, dialogue-based interactions (e.g., executive coaching, counseling, and motivational interviewing).

The core ingredients of a healthy interpersonal springboard are

- empathy
- building or support of self-confidence
- compassion or demonstration of understanding
- nonjudgmental feedback
- mutual exchange of information

To the extent that the interviewer can act and react in a manner that enhances these elements, the interviewer is working effectively to build rapport.

For instance, state "your resume is extremely impressive, I've especially noted your experience in diverse industries—was that a goal of yours, to work across industries or did that happen by chance?" rather than ... "Please tell me about your cross industry experience and why you think it is important." In other circumstances, "you impress me as a considerate person, how exactly did you get involved with this mess?"

It is how you ask a question, not merely the words but what you seem to emphasize, care about, or focus on that matter. In the aforementioned career example, the interviewer demonstrates a sense of value for the individual's career path—the interviewee will feel appreciated and is given the opportunity to respond in kind—being thoughtful, warm, and open. Failure for the interviewee to respond in kind is important assessment information.

3. Action Item

Listen more and talk less.

Rationale

Listening and gathering information from others provides you with clues to help evaluate the situation and the person. Whether you are interviewing a potential client, a job applicant, a subordinate, or mentoring a protégé, the information collected is useless if you don't fully digest it. That means active listening. You can't address a problem, learn a need, or explore a person if you don't let the information in.

The interviewee should spend more time talking than the interviewer. The interviewer should allow the interviewee to discuss and elaborate. This is most productive by asking open-ended questions that allow the person to talk freely. Open ended does not imply useless or nondirective. Open ended does mean a lack of structure. A protocol of open-ended questions can be standardized (so all interviews are conducted using the same questions) and metrics can be created to aid in the evaluation of responses using criteria mapped to the purpose of the interview.

> "Tell me why you think you are a good fit"
> "What differentiates you from others applying for this job?"
> "What do you bring that is valuable to us?"
> "Why do you want to work here, rather than do this type of work elsewhere?"

This course of action also provides you with information for asking additional questions to uncover the person's needs, abilities, or deficits. Inherent in this is that you guide the person in talking about relevant issues, situations, or opportunities. This requires not only asking the right questions, but also listening actively so that follow-up questions can be asked.

4. Action Item

Assume accountability for establishing rapport.

Rationale

Interviewees, for the most part, are in a responsive and not a proactive mode. As the one in control, the interviewer must be accountable for attempting to develop rapport. There are many ways to do so but the bottom-line is to make the interviewee comfortable, relaxed, and open the interview with light conversation. Skilled interviewers do this in a manner that feels genuine to the interviewee. That is, the conversation or questions don't appear "forced to provoke rapport" if you will. The inexperienced will ask three questions rapidly as if getting them out of the way and the questions are often generic. By the manner of asking, it becomes painfully obvious that the interviewer is not really interested in the response and right away the interview is headed in the wrong direction.

Begin interviews by being polite and respectful. Be careful about monitoring your first impressions and not letting irrelevant factors influence how you proceed (e.g., information on paper and appearance). Throw the person a compliment about their background since you've studied their resume. Make them feel welcomed. If you find that this is difficult for you to do, then think about why you are interviewing the person and to what extent you are acting for or against the interview's purpose.

A large software development company was hiring for a senior organization development position. Greetings were politely exchanged. The candidate removed his coat and hat and sat down although was not offered a seat. The interview began with a quick "did you find us okay?" followed by "I only have 40 minutes for you" and soon moved to "if I like you I will want you to sit for a battery of tests." The seasoned professional responded by pausing (to enable the interviewer to slow down, focus, and attend to the situation at hand) and when the interviewer finally looked at the candidate in the eye—the candidate wisely responded, "Where's my hat?"

In this scenario, the interview was a failure from the start because the interviewer, so intensely focused on personal needs (and with little self-awareness) thought little of (or about) the interviewee and offered a perfunctory rapport-building performance. The assessment of the interviewer by the interviewee was negative and led to an immediate dismissal of the opportunity.

Failure to develop rapport by the interviewer causes the demise of the exchange. Poor rapport may be a sign of disinterest, confusion, deception, or some other unattractive interpersonal quality. Again, these are harsh and immediate discoveries that affect (if not define) the quality of the interview. Furthermore, the interviewee is collecting information about the nature of the interviewer and likely the organization and the culture the interviewer reflects. Is this organization sterile, impersonal, and uncaring just like its interview process?

The onus is on the interviewer to build rapport so the stage can be set for an effective discovery of the interviewee.

Try some things:

- Ask questions that are related to the forthcoming interview, but are easy to answer.
- Express appreciation for the interviewee's time.
- Smile, make good eye contact, care about the conversation.

- Focus on making the individual comfortable (unless discomfort is staged for job-relevant reasons).
- Keep a to-do list handy regarding rapport in addition to the structured interview guide.

5. Action Item

Foster a climate that welcomes expression.

Rationale

The interview is a medium for expression—expression of knowledge, skills, abilities, personal characteristics, and interests.

The effective interviewer ensures that the expression of the interviewee is not inhibited. It is the responsibility of the interviewer to ensure that there is nothing in the way of expression. It is easy to shut down communication; not so easy to open it up.

Avoid rapid, blunt delivery. A structured interview or prewritten interview protocol (i.e., a standardized list of questions that enables a comparison between responses) does not need to be delivered like an automaton. Automatons do not breed thoughtful responses or invite expression from others. The ineffective interviewer creates an interviewee who is evasive or reserved or confined when, in fact, the individual is merely trying to comply or conform to the expectations of the interviewer. Blunt or curt questions imply a desire for blunt, curt answers. Interviewers get what they give.

Match the interview context to its purpose by focusing not only what is asked but how it is asked as well. Factor the amount of time available for the interview and if time is pressured—tell the interviewee this up front. This enables the interviewee to respond with both time and the question in mind.

If you are expecting to identify whether the interviewee can speak informally then don't ask formal questions, in a formal style and in an abrupt manner. That's not playing fair and everybody loses—assessment is inaccurate. Don't limit or define how expression "should occur" and then evaluate results as if you are not actively impacting the expression.

In a subject matter or knowledge-driven interview, the interviewer states at the get-go that he only has 30 minutes to ascertain the interviewee's technical competence. The interviewee responds to questions concisely, sometimes in generalities offering to go into details only if the interviewer requests so. The interviewee is trying to hit hard with blunt answers while demonstrating sensitivity for interview time requirements and politely offering to go into details (eating more time) only by request. Because the context of the interview is crafted and shared with the interviewee, the evaluation of technical expertise is accurate. Expression is influenced by the context of the interview created by the interviewer.

6. Action Item

Realize that body language of the interviewer impacts interview outcomes.

Rationale

There are hosts of popular books on "body language" that purport to know the secrets of reading body cues. It's not so easy to infer psychological states or motivations from body motion (or lack thereof). To draw inferences about motivations, interests, or personality based on body cues alone is a mistake. If you find yourself wondering about a motivational state based on a body cue, always test what you suspect. You must gather objective evidence to validate your inference. Lob some "trial balloons" or follow-up questions to probe, inspect, or confirm that which you suspect.

Cues other than spoken words are important aspects of the interview. Use them to your advantage by incorporating them into follow-up or probing questions. Remain focused on gathering behavioral, objective evidence to support the inferences you draw.

Interviewers must present themselves as engaged, interested, and involved or else they risk the privilege to access the interviewee. Proxemics tells us that personal space can be used to affect behavior and the body cues of the interviewer (motion, distance, intensity) can be used to establish the context in which you'd like to observe what a person says or does.

Beware of drawing inferences based on body language of the interviewee. Though, at times, some physical movements can be used to suggest hidden psychological states, it's best to validate this inference using structured questions and probing—find alignment between what is stated. Seek reliability in the past behavioral examples you collect and the physicality you are witnessing.

At best, use body movements to develop hypotheses about the interviewee that require testing. As an exception to the "beware body movement" warning, there is a formidable literature and practice based on the interpretation of micro-expressions and facial movement to infer emotion (see the work of Paul Ekman). Before you tackle micro-expressions, stand warned that while research in this area is formidable, the practice of identification and interpretation of imperceptible facial movements during the interview is not something that can likely be easily acquired.

7. Action Item

Assess authenticity by observing open and expressive manner.

Rationale

Interviewees who convey "canned" messages are not offering authenticity. They are scripted because they cannot speak from personal depth or can't think on their feet or they "come in" ready to *present* a self rather than *be* themselves. Untruthful (or "close to the vest") communications tend to be short and rigid. However, lengthy, verbose, unnecessary explanations offered as a defensive strategy are not likely indicative of honesty.

Interviewees who "present" themselves in a personal, engaged style—not relying on a script—are generally affable, likeable, and build good rapport rapidly. The difference between a genuine individual and one who is "protected" is most apparent in rapport or lack thereof. This happens early in the interview. Bad rapport is a bad sign.

Be careful disliking interviewees who are genuine because they are somewhat wordy or don't walk and talk like a "proverbial elevator speech." Those quoting great thinkers regularly, communicating like a corporate power point presentation or never getting "off story," are tightly packaged. The strong suit of such individuals is likely an empty suit.

On the basis of experience, individuals who speak openly, pause and think and provide explanations or elaborate freely are easier to learn from, are more open to sharing information, and generally are more willing to place the needs of others ahead of themselves. Of course, if you are looking to ensure "fit" for a closed, tightly controlled, environment of automatons then the walking power point might be a good choice.

Application of this very point appeared during a succession planning engagement. Senior managers were interviewed and provided a development plan by a firm of consulting psychologists. On the list of competencies was ethics. The interviewer asked one senior manager for his personal view of ethics and the response came verbatim from the corporate handbook—another internal candidate waxed on the interaction of personality, corporate culture, and social pressures that impact behavior and how individuals can (and should) resist the push for doing wrong.

Clearly, the latter candidate spends more time thinking about and likely controlling personal behavior. Always pick the genuine, more open talker over the canned program. Beware of information that seem incomplete, it likely is—though you may not know why. When you suspect a problem, ask again, probe, and don't "settle" for a non-answer, a half-answer, or an answer that contradicts an earlier response. All of these interview situations can be rich sources of additional information if you pause and spend the time to mine them.

Try these, for instance:

"I don't understand exactly what you did in that situation, can you describe it to me again?"

"When you say, you don't recall exactly—go ahead and share what you do recall, please."

"I am confused, based on what you told me earlier, what you just expressed seems like a contradiction. Can you help me with that?"

"I don't have a good understanding yet. Let's go back to my first question, can you tell me again what the situation was and how you handled it?"

8. Action Item

Conduct intense assessments in a nonthreatening manner.

Rationale

Interviews for jobs of high consequence or high stakes (e.g., protective services, law enforcement, quality control, and CEO) are best conducted in a manner that opens the interviewee so that a look at their values, interests, and focus is apparent. A tactic that opens interviewees rapidly is to demonstrate acceptance as soon as possible. This will reduce "masking" so you can gain access to the real person behind the interviewee.

A "friendly" style diminishes the perception of threat and reduces the need to overcome resistance (as there is little) toward discussing difficult or critical circumstances in the interviewee's past experiences. Questions about past behavior are instead viewed as interesting and can be positioned to flatter the interviewee.

A corporate executive placement example:

> "You've been in situations that led to exponential market growth and you've also led business units that dissolved. This is quite a stretch. What did you learn from these experiences that will be useful to you in the role of CEO in a turnaround situation?"

Another example, interviewing law enforcement officers applying for assignments in conflict-laden territories around the world:

> "You've got an impressive background reducing the likelihood of violence in difficult situations. What is your secret? Perhaps you can walk me through a situation that could have gone bad but didn't and then walk me through a situation that did in fact 'go bad'—tell me about your role in these circumstances—*help me learn* what goes on in the mind of a professional handling such terrible circumstances."

The challenge here is to unlock the individual so they want to inform, educate, or reveal. By asking them to elaborate on specific situations and being respectful of what they know (and experienced)—reduces the level of interviewer threat and the candidate's willingness to share motivations, actions, and outcomes is much improved.

Safe environments breed more information than threatening environments. Interviewers can obtain more information through flattery than flagellation. An example of this follows.

In screening candidates for private security work in conflict-laden territories worldwide, a candidate is complimented about his work history handling sensitive interpersonal matters in a highly diverse territory. The follow-up to this compliment (backed by a stellar 17-year performance record) was the question "how do you handle the badgering or taunting of people—we all know it happens, especially in roles of authority—yet your record is impeccable. How do you manage to handle people that get in your face?"

The question is posed softly and as if nothing else is more important than to learn from the interviewee. Sincerity. The candidate softly answers back, as if making certain that no one else can hear the response. This peaks the interviewer's interest since a secret is about to be revealed. The candidate says, "I step on their toes." The interviewer says nothing not knowing if this is a literal or figurative expression. The candidate adds "if I can force them to make a bolder, unlawful physical move—once they touch me ... then I can make them mine" (i.e., uses physical tactics to take down, cuff, and call the authorities for formal arrest). This provocative interpersonal tactic was shared with pride and gleam. How the interviewer set-up the question was as important as the question itself.

To investigate or probe the interviewer should

- facilitate openness
- be supportive
- be nonthreatening
- demonstrate a desire to learn
- ask the interviewee to help you, so you can understand better, more fully
- shift perceived control of the interview to the interviewee
- control your facial expressions (don't reward or punish responses)

This is a winning combination that enables access to personal competencies especially when assessing individuals for high-stakes positions such as in law enforcement, protective services, or other high-consequence jobs.

9. Action Item

Disclose to encourage disclosure.

Rationale

It is difficult to bring people to deep conversations by asking questions especially under time constraints. The interviewee might be uncertain about whether you really want them to discuss something on a topic that is not often disclosed or perhaps there could be personal discomfort with disclosure itself.

It is however often very important to know the person's values, life experiences, and overall character. Mining for such information is hazardous work but the increasingly detrimental impact of unethical, selfish, or uncaring motivations on businesses and people is becoming profoundly evident (i.e., Worldcom, Tyco, and Enron).

The difficulty in obtaining meaningful information about intricacies of a person's values lies in paving the way to the information. The interviewer must make the revealing of personal insights legitimate and desirable. Risk is assumed when disclosure occurs. The interviewer must enable the interviewee to assume that risk. The interviewee does not necessarily need to be comfortable with this risk—but they do, nonetheless, need to assume it.

An effective means to enabling personal disclosure is to model such behavior. For instance, following a set of legitimate but "light" interview questions, pause for a moment and explain your interest in knowing the character of the people you are to bring into the firm or otherwise need to know. Legitimize the fact that character and values are core to knowing people and that "really" getting to know the person is what you value most. Far beyond "competencies" or skills or other such matters, disclosure about personal values, difficult choices, or meaningful life experiences can bring forth a depth that "competencies" (i.e., skill and ability-linked job-related characteristics) don't usually touch.

As the interviewer, you are in control and you set expectations for what is to be discussed, so self-disclose to invite self-disclosure. This can be easily segued by telling a relevant story and offering what you learned. Be selective, be relevant to the job or purpose of the interview, and demonstrate personal depth. Don't shy away from offering a mistake or a lesson learned or even a misjudgment or mistake you made. Lead the interviewee on a path to self-discovery by taking him/her by the hand if necessary. Show the interviewee what you want to know about him/her by sharing information about yourself at the same level of depth.

Engaged interviewees respond to the disclosures of others easily. Disclosure is experienced as a positive, healthy process and warrants little resistance once enabled. Responsive disclosure reflects good interpersonal skills and a level of comfort and self-awareness that are likely positive features. Utilize access to information that is useful to the prediction of behavior in circumstances that call for distinctive sets of character, values, and ethical principles. Use disclosure as a data-mining tool.

10. Action Item

Form an alliance to improve interview outcomes.

Rationale

To facilitate rapport and also enable access to information you require, create an alliance. Alliances are productive, constructive, and not intimidating. Alliances lead to useful outcomes for all parties involved. Alliances are healthy interpersonal influences.

Alliances are positive and are enabled by interviewer behavior that

- shows acceptance
- is attentive
- is respectful
- demonstrates warmth
- is nonjudgmental (listening)
- is emotionally available
- is genuine

Use vocabulary that is fitting—don't purposely talk over someone's head or for that matter be patronizing. Do what is comfortable for you, but take into consideration the background, educational level, and information you are assessing at the moment to form a communication style that will work.

This communication style is about enhancing a sense of comfort or acceptance—don't play act; don't be what you are not but do take into consideration the verbal skills and needs of others to select your words, pace, and style in a way that is accepting. It is critical that your communication be genuine, however. Good interviewers are flexible communicators, good self-monitors, and a quick-read for the needs of others.

Generally, people open more quickly and will be more honest once an alliance is formed. Alliances however are challenged by many factors including perceived differences or threats. Overcome adversity in the interview situation by getting close. The interviewer assumes accountability for establishing an alliance.

No one wants to be alone. There is a human tendency to connect, at least on some level, for most people. This affords an opportunity from which, with probing and warmth, you can form an alliance. It is a way to accept the person to whom you are speaking and therefore exchange information, engage in dialogue.

Even in noninterrogative interviews, initially, there is a wall separating the interviewer and the interviewee. The extent to which this wall blocks communication is a measure of interviewer failure.

Connecting at a humanistic or compassionate level opens the interviewee. People want to be heard, understood, forgiven, challenged or are driven to dialogue for some other need. Addressing this need makes it possible, always, to create an alliance on some basis and therefore open the floodgates to useful dialogue.

The quintessential good–bad investigator scenario is familiar to many where the person being interviewed "reaches out" to the interviewer who understands—thwarting the bad interviewer to whom they feel no attachment. Dialogue ensues because an alliance is formed.

11. Action Item

Encourage openness by being nonjudgmental.

Rationale

To facilitate rapport and also enable access to information you require, be more like the person you are interviewing than unlike them. This "similarity" tactic can be leveraged on multiple scales. The way you sit—make it similar to the way the interviewee sits. Use vocabulary that is fitting—don't do what is very uncomfortable for you, but pick words, metaphors—communicate in a way that connects to the person you hope to address. Go where they are to communicate effectively. This communication style is about enhancing a sense of comfort or acceptance—don't play act; don't be what you are not, but do take into consideration the verbal skills and needs of others to select your words, pace, and style in a way that communicates comfort or acceptance.

Generally, people will open more quickly and will be more honest when not under threat. Sometimes "differences" are threatening or at least can be perceived to be so (rightly or wrongly). Differences can be sparked by economic disparities, authority or power differentials, cultural gaps, accents, as well as any other characteristic that an individual views as significant to them. This is a phenomenological reality—it resides in the head of the interviewee, but it is real, it is experienced, and it impacts (or can impact) the effectiveness of the interviewer. (Indeed, inferences prompted by differences can reside in the head of the interviewee as well, leading to affecting interview outcomes.)

Overcome the challenges of disparity by getting close subtly. There is a fine yet clear line between speaking like the person you are attempting to engage (vocabulary, pace of speech) and patronizing others. Be aware of communication differences and use it to your advantage. For most, these differences are easily noticeable—so if speech is very different—asking for clarification might be a good idea rather than assuming your communication is understood, for instance. Slowing your pace (or speeding it up) could make you more effective. Open yourself to feedback so you can communicate more effectively. Needless to say, in the global economy, cross-cultural communication is critical and this reality extends to the interview. Communication is key and the interviewer assumes accountability for ensuring that the message sent and the message received is accurate.

When probing to gain further insight, inform the interviewee about what you would be thinking if you were in their shoes—you articulate their world and share how you might act or feel in similar situations. Your words describe the world as they see it. You display understanding. They open up.

12. Action Item

Demonstrate patience.

Rationale

While most interviewers testify that they are focused on technical or structural aspects of the interview, often the singular element that interferes with good assessment is adhering to the structure alone—and ignoring the intangibles of the conversation, especially the need for patience. Effective interviewers are skilled at knowing when to interrupt and when to listen.

The interviewer launches a well-thought out, complicated question that is delivered proudly. Unfortunately, the interviewer is spending too much time thinking about the great question formulated—and not enough time focusing on the response. Instead, the interviewer is mentally unavailable to the interviewee and though unaware, focuses on the next question to ask on the structured protocol. The result is that

1. the interviewer does not realize that a great question requires a thoughtful, articulated response
2. the interviewer is annoyed with a response that is "taking away" from the attention (and pride) felt by asking terrific questions (the interviewee is, in a sense, "stealing the stage")
3. the interviewer misjudges the interviewee's competence
4. the interviewer's narcissism overpowers the purpose of the interview
5. the utility of the structured interview is squandered by a lack of patience

Thoughtful responses to interview questions require time and energy. Let the interviewee speak and properly appreciate the time and energy being put into the answer. This demands interviewer patience. If impatience is getting the better of you, try this:

- If you want a brief answer, then ask for it.
- If the interviewee is pondering in silence, ask them to share their thoughts.
- Say "please tell me what are you thinking"—you'd be surprised what you learn by discovering how information is being crafted, filtered, or prepared for you.

The process by which people "construct" their responses can reveal invaluable information (sometimes more valuable than the response itself). Interviewers who are more self-focused than other-focused reduce information exchange. This can be overcome by demonstrating patience. Patience and self-awareness enable you to ask better questions, at the right time, and bring newfound opportunities to learn and truly understand what the interviewee is saying (beyond merely capturing words spoken).

13. Action Item

Use probes to aid memory when expected information is not forthcoming.

Rationale

There are many obstacles to gaining access to information. The interviewer must maximize the information collected, minimize contamination, and maintain the integrity of the assessment process. The structure of the interview guides the content and sampling of subject matter or "competencies" (personal characteristics) to be assessed. Skill makes it possible to find, release, and capture the information you want.

Prime the interviewee to improve memory and strengthen the pathway to the information you want. The priming of the interviewee overcomes contamination (unwanted or useless information) and therefore enhances the value of the question you ask. The interviewee may be resisting or not recalling the information you seek. So, pose it differently, repeatedly, and capitalize on all sense memory systems—recall if information is based on emotion, time sequences, colors, weather, emotional states, and other contextual aspects of the information (or event)—deploy these in the questions you ask.

- Do ask for behavioral specifics ("What exactly were you thinking at the time?" "Was your heart beating quickly at the time, tell me about it").
- Optimize recall by asking questions using investigative tactics to enhance memory.

    "Can you describe the situation beginning with the last thing you remember?"

    "Can you describe what it was like to handle the situational emotionally?"

    "What was your emotional state at the time, how were you feeling, and what did you see or say at that time?"

    "Can you tell me the single aspect of the situation that really stands out in your mind as you attacked the problem?"
- Reveal the presence or absence of a competency by overcoming irrelevant obstacles such as anxiety, a desire to please, or feeling threatened or overwhelmed by the interview situation (note: if managing anxiety is relevant to the assessment, then, of course, this behavior is important).
- Tell the individual to "go back in time" for past event recall. Ask about who was present, if olfactory elements were present at the time, resurface them as well. Invite recollection of multisensory information to enhance recall about targeted information related by time and place.
- If recall is linked to an emotional state, then take the individual to that state to improve recall. Information recall is better when recalling that information in the same emotional state as when learned. Take the interviewee to emotional states that may be conducive to memory. In general, information that is negative in nature is better recalled when in a similar state of mind as when first learned (or experienced).

14. Action Item

Nurture the giving of negative information by putting down the pen and relaxing.

Rationale

The best way to bring forth critical information is to not reveal to the interviewee that they are in the process of informing you of something vital. Assuming the information is unflattering to the interviewee or otherwise critical to the assessment process, it is a mistake to put your nose to your legal pad and take copious notes—do not signal a counterproductive alarm.

The exposure of negative information often comes when unexpected or when the interviewee is "thinking aloud"—if not rambling. Although you are taking notes throughout the interview—do not do a nosedive into your legal pad when critical negative information is placed on the table. Instead, put the pen down as if to go into a "chat" mode—demonstrating casualness, informality, and anything but criticality.

Note-taking is important of course but it can be intimidating to people wanting to not disclose, deceive, or otherwise play things close to the vest. The very visible act of placing the pen down (relaxing) and leaning back in the interview chair can bring a sense of "safeness" to the interviewer serving to catalyze the giving of critical information. Alternatively, demonstrating a focus, concern, or intensity on information being revealed will shut down the concerned interviewee.

It is also important that you validate the information you are collecting. Get the facts, the specifics. There is some risk in that you pay attention to negative or unflattering remarks rather than more bland or positive bits of information. This could subtly reinforce or encourage the giving of such information. Care must be taken to not unduly influence the direction of the interview while also making certain that the interviewee is "free" to give the information you need.

For example, during an interview of a middle-level manager as part of high-potential assessment (i.e., succession planning process), information about "frustrations when managing" was not revealed until the interviewer shared his own frustrations about managing (when in a corporate position) and the two had a good laugh. With the pen down and the interview being more jovial than serious, the interviewee shared how he disliked managing and that he had serious doubts about being responsible for a business unit or for taking on profit and loss responsibility. This was uncovered just as the interviewer was about to say "thank you and good-bye."

15. Action Item

Share what you are thinking if you need help connecting the dots.

Rationale

Interviews are purposeful. They are not random events. There may be different reasons for interviews, but they all are conducted to get at information that leads to the making of judgments or decisions.

Despite best efforts it is possible that, as the interviewer, you remain uncertain or unclear about a candidate's interest, values, or capabilities. You've asked a variety of questions and yet, for some unknown reason, you remain uncertain or unconvinced.

Face the unknown head on!

It is not a weakness to inform the candidate that you are having difficulty. Many, in the interviewer seat, strive to demonstrate their prowess. Omniscience is a lofty goal—put it away; it doesn't belong in the interview. Instead, gain power by giving up power.

Ask the candidate:

- I am not entirely sure why you are interested in this assignment.
- I am having a difficult time understanding how you made decisions when investing other people's money.
- You do not make me entirely confident in your statements.
- Tell me again why this venture is important to you.
- Would you explain your decision to leave that employer once again.

Asking the interviewee to help you with "closure" activates the individual. The burden for the lack of understanding is shifted from you—onto them—and, as a result, new, useful information is generated.

16. Action Item

Uncover self-image and related perceptions by asking candidates to describe themselves in situations experienced or to-be experienced.

Rationale

People have fairly clear self-images and can easily capture essential features of these representations in a list of adjectives. Assess how people see themselves by relying on visual information—how they literally view themselves in certain situations. Emphasize the interviewee's need to describe themselves in handling or managing specific situations—obtain adjectives and behavioral examples.

Ask visual questions that touch emotional and behavioral nerves:

"Imagine a time or picture yourself when making a presentation to the board of directors of a global consumer products company ... how does that feel? What are you (were you) thinking? What would you do? How would you get ready?"

"Tell me about a time when you had to (imagine yourself needing to) correct the behavior of a direct report (alternate peer, colleague, boss)—what did you do, what was that like, how did you handle it?"

"Think about a conflict situation you needed to handle—preferably with your boss or a significant person in your life. How did you approach the problem? Walk me through your experience and describe how you felt, about the situation and about yourself."

The particular qualities contained in each person's list of adjectives and behavioral descriptions capture their unique self-image, sense of self-esteem and confidence, as well as certain ways they wish to be perceived by others—relative to the situation certainly, but possibly transportable to other situations or circumstances. Self-images internalize from experience with key figures in life. They offer important clues to previous mentoring experiences, success, and failures and future mentoring needs. Self-images can teach about how the person learns, adapts, and grows. Self-images offer rich avenues to assess potential for a given specific job or challenge.

Relying on visuals and adjectives enables a quick sketch of client self-perception. Personal traits are reflected clearly in each person's adjective and behavioral list and offer possibilities for an assessment of how this person might fit in as an individual or team member in a particular work or social setting.

17. Action Item

Obtain facts by being open and personable, warm, and to-the-point.

Rationale

It is often necessary to set aside one's desire to hear an answer, and nothing but the answer, to our questions. Patience is called for under fact-finding circumstances and a genuine interest in the interviewee is advantageous. This sometimes means setting aside your focus on getting the answer to your question and instead using your question as a means to access the information you want. The interview is not a verbal paper-and-pencil quiz.

Thinking that a structured interview requires "to the point" responses in a specified amount of time is self-defeating. Although we may be looking for an answer to fit into a box, or a specific category, the interviewee may not be operating under the same heuristic. The very questions we ask may unleash memories and experiences that result in meandering. To dismiss the interviewee's desire to share important emotions or observations because it "isn't on your interview scorecard" is foolish, perceived to-be disrespectful, and is self-destructive. Interview quality suffers as a result as does the data collected.

For example, a list of structured questions was compiled along with a rating scale to assess the responses of a team of emergency managers handling a crisis. Responses to specific, factual questions resulted in "Did I tell you about the hurricane of '02? I was soaking wet, filthy, hadn't slept in two days, bugs everywhere, winds ripping through the camp ..."

An initial reaction to this recital might be a desire to scream "Stop—just answer my question." But the interviewee *is* answering your question. The interviewee, by way of storytelling, is sharing, sorting, and recalling information that is helpful to memory and bringing comfort or preparedness to address a question. Once this is done, the answer needed can be accessed and delivered to the interviewer.

To get the interviewee to listen to you, and answer your questions, allow the interviewee to answer in the manner or method that makes sense to them—not your scorecard, protocol, or structured interview checklist. Place interpersonal and memory recall needs ahead of your note-taking priorities. Then, capture the behavioral information you need.

18. Action Item

Ask open-ended questions to get interviewee to talk more.

Rationale

Interviews often contain two types of questions: open-ended and closed. Open-ended questions invite the interviewee to explain or expand on a topic. An example of this is, "Tell me about your previous job experience." Closed questions address very specific types of information and often can be answered in a word or two. An example is, "How long have you been working in this field?" Interviewers typically create an interview guide that includes a mixture of open and closed questions because it improves the flow of interviews, and provides more give-and-take between the interviewer and interviewee.

For example, if the interview question is about job experience, a question such as, "What job experience have you had?" may invite shy interviewees to provide a list of job titles and tasks associated with these tasks. A good follow-up question brief reply would be, "Tell me about what you did at those jobs." This encourages the interviewee to expand on his or her responses.

Similarly, sometimes interviewees are long-winded, or take up much interview time on a single topic; these interviewees can often be redirected by asking a closed question. So in answer to the same question, "What job experience have you had?" an interviewee may provide excruciating detail regarding each of his or her past 12 jobs. A follow-up question to limit the voluminous response might be, "In the last job you had, what three skills were most important?"

These techniques can also be used for individuals who are expressing emotionality that the interviewer would like to moderate; closed questions will serve to limit and constrain emotional expression; open-ended questions will serve to encourage it.

19. Action Item

Trigger memory by allowing free association.

Rationale

To gather information recount events, step by step. The reasons are simple. When information is recalled, each memory builds on the last. Whereas it might seem that facts can be gathered in an abrupt "dragnet" style of questions, the reality is that allowing the interviewee freedom enables the collection of facts more effectively than "deposition" style attacks. Allowing freedom in the expression of memory facilitates information gathering.

Gather information in an orderly progression, start from the beginning. An effective method is to ask "What did you do?" "Why did you do that?" "What did you do next?" If more detail is required, or if you do not understand what was said, ask the interviewee to elaborate, using a phrase such as "Please explain, tell me more about." Such questions allow the interviewee to respond in his or her own words. Never ask: "Did you follow the rules?" "Did you do what you were supposed to?" Clearly, the response will be closed and abrupt and likely what you expect to hear.

Orderly progression can begin from any starting point that makes sense to the interviewee. "What is the first thing that comes to mind when you recall the incident? What comes to mind after that?" Alternatively, "walk me through the situation starting with the last thing that happened and work backwards or if you prefer tell me about what you remember best, to get started." It is key to offer some level of structure accompanied by freedom to recall in a manner that makes sense to the interviewee. This can be useful even in the context of the employment interview where you are asking the candidate to walk-through a complex project such as an enterprise-wide implementation (e.g., enterprise resource planning initiative) or when asking a seasoned professional for a stroll through their job progressions and decisions made during their career.

When asking questions, try the simple phrase "Tell me, in your own words, what you did, when you did it, and why."

20. Action Item

Be alert for emotional expressions when none are expected.

Rationale

It is easy to forget that a topic innocuous to one person is possibly provocative for another.

Any topic, no matter how harmless you think it is, can elicit emotion—anger, sadness, despair, shame, guilt. Asking simple questions can bring waves of memories, or the recall of experiences either wonderful or horrid. The interviewer never knows what lies beneath the surface of an apparently bland question. Besides being potentially open to legal challenge for discrimination in a selection interview, asking "How many children do you have?" can spawn memories of tremendous grief to a parent experienced in child loss or it can summon enormous pride for the parent celebrating a child's first birthday. So, for both legal reasons in the employment context and emotional reasons in another context, interviewers should be sensitive toward and responsive to reactions from questions asked.

While interviewing corporate security officers for high-risk assignments in Bosnia, the interviewer asks, "Why do you want the job?" and stumbles upon a personal history of child abuse and a desire to make the world better for a child somewhere. Interviewers need to be alert, compassionate, directive, and respectful. Simple, structured questions can evoke complex, loose emotions. Be careful you don't ignore the need for interpersonal acumen by leaning too heavily on a structured interview to do the work. Be alert, perceptive—keep your radar on for verbal and nonverbal responses. Stay awake and monitor emotion.

At casual glance, we do not know what occurred in a person's life. When you ask a question, pay careful attention to the affective reactions it may elicit. Realize that the sensitivity of the question may not be known to you—or knowable, for that matter. Back off if you sense that you have strayed into forbidden (unnecessary) territory. Move forward strategically if the information is relevant to the assessment. Above all, respect each person's individuality and do not judge—but do not ignore, should the emotion open doors to legitimate areas of assessment.

21. Action Item

Benefit from the interview to assess personality even if you are also using written tests.

Rationale

Personality measures are related to key business outcomes, such as leadership, training success, and job performance. They are also related to counterproductive work behaviors such as absenteeism, health care costs, accidents and injuries, and conflict. Personality is the ultimate "fit" measure, often being the pivotal basis for personnel decisions.

Interviews can add important additional predictive power to hiring and placement decisions over and above self-report measures of personality alone (personality tests are inventories, a series of questions, that individuals answer to describe themselves, these inventories offer psychometric reliability and validity). Since both interviews and personality tests can be useful, interviewer judgments of personality provide a more complete picture of the candidate than personality tests alone.

Self-report personality tests are more susceptible to inflation (exaggeration) than interviews. Often, organizations use "tests" that are biased, unfair, invalid, or "pretend" to be personality tests but they lack empirical backbone. Solid, research-based personality tests typically require a licensed psychologist (to order, administer, and interpret)—not something that is practical internally. Nonetheless, many "tests" are out there. Caveat emptor.

Examples of personality measures that can be assessed in an interview:

Altruism: the extent to which an individual is generous, considerate, and willing to help others.

Self-discipline: the extent to which an individual is motivated to get the job done and follows through on tasks despite boredom and distractions.

Initiative: the conscientious, deliberate execution of an initiative over time that yields an outcome.

Vulnerability: the extent to which an individual is able to cope with stressful events.

For example, to measure vulnerability, an interviewer could ask: "We all have had times when the pressure at work is extremely high. Tell me about a time when you had several competing deadlines or had a very important project that had high stakes attached. Describe how you felt. How did you deal with the situation?"

Personality research established the Big Five factors—these are useful dimensions for many purposes not limited to selection, promotion, and developmental planning. The five dimensions are (a) neuroticism (level of worry or concern), (b) extraversion (preference to deal with the external world in relation to being introspective), (c) openness to new experiences (propensity to learn or experience novel things), (d) conscientiousness (a sense of diligence), and (e) agreeableness (being affable, personable, nonargumentative). These dimensions are measurable using written tests (e.g., California Psychological Inventory, Jackson

Personality Inventory, Hogan, and NEO-Personality Inventory) as well as using structured, behavioral interviews (using past and future-oriented) questions.

22. Action Item

Assess intelligence or cognitive ability during the interview to improve predictions about potential/performance and usefulness of information collected.

Rationale

General cognitive ability remains a predictor of success and analytic skills implicate potential in general. Critical thinking and the ability to decipher what information to use and how to use it are competencies that generalize these abilities to enhance performance in many situations. In addition, information collected based on the digestion or reasoning of an individual whose analytical ability is deficient must be further questioned or verified before the information offered can be accepted as factual. Of course, from a phenomenological perspective, an individual's explanation or worldview is in and of itself useful, but only in that regard. To assess cognitive ability, ask future-oriented or hypothetical questions such as "How would you go about solving a problem where …" or "How would you go about handling a situation where …"

Future-oriented, hypothetical, situational questions are a terrific way to gain information about cognitive ability especially useful when the interviewee may not offer past relevant experience from which to sample. Of course, while intelligence is important for understanding and solving complex problems, interviewers (in employment situations) to be neglectful to focus on pure analytical aptitude without deference to the findings of a job analysis, which will have indicated the actual competencies necessary for success. It is worth mentioning that competencies should be broken down into behavior-specific definitions as a rule of thumb for assessment.

To assess cognitive skills, be sure to ask questions that reflect analytical capability. Remember that "raw intelligence" and constructs like "emotional intelligence" are not the same and likely deserve equal attention (recall that the competencies or behaviorally defined requirements should be drawn from an analysis of the situation or job, that is, the job analysis). Interpersonal acumen, the intelligence necessary to read, decipher, and react to social situations effectively require questions focused specifically on those behavioral elements.

Much training and attention is given to human resource professionals and recruiters where the emphasis is on "ask about past, job-relevant events so that you can record objective behaviors"—this is a fine principle but just because questions are specific and ask about behaviors doesn't mean that they will derive information that is useful in inferring cognitive ability. Remember memory is a creative construction. Waxing on the past is a reconstruction of what a person chooses to remember (or create) and is able to convey (overcoming verbal challenges and perhaps emotional challenges that come with sharing prior unpleasant experiences).

The responses to behavior-specific questions are often useful in inferring motivation and conscientiousness (or other job-related competencies) rather than cognitive ability. To evaluate ability, the questions need to dig into why a person made certain choices, walk-through an example of what a person did, how they made decisions—get a feel for how they "ascertain" what matters and how they go about acting (or not) upon information gathered.

Are they thinking logically? Do they weigh the pros and cons? Do they factor in the complexity? They can translate difficult or complex information into simple language? Can they explain a complex situation to you in a way that is easy to understand?

Here are some examples of questions that reveal cognitive complexity:

"Tell me about how you would manage the implementation of a plan to reorganize the sales division."

"If you were given the responsibility to restructure the southwest region, what might you do first? Why?"

"How would you go about learning the best way to differentiate our firm?"

"Consider the high-potential individuals you identified in your previous leadership assignments, tell me what you used as key indicators? What factors worked for you or against you in making good judgments about people?"

"I understand you are seasoned in constructing valid, behaviorally objective, structured interviews. In this job, you will need to supervise all selection practices for the organization. Can you explain to me how you would go about making certain that our hiring practices are legally and professionally sound?"

23. Action Item

Utilize standardized professional instrumentation complemented by behavioral question protocols to improve information gathering, especially for personality assessment.

Rationale

When the goal is personality assessment, it is best to be evidence based. Evidence can be easily integrated from various sources using different methods. Integrated assessment of personality is better than singular or one-context samples.

Personality is typically an important element of most interview scenarios, albeit for different purposes. The assessment of personality however is often not only the outcome of an interview but it is also an element that either "leaks into" or influences the interview process covertly or directly impacts how the interviewer asks a question and even what questions are asked.

The personality of the interviewee affects what questions you ask and how you ask them. This can influence the interviewer from the "get-go" and often (inexperienced) interviewers strive to develop a rapport not realizing the degree of accommodation or changes in style required. The interviewee's personality will require interviewer adjustment. Experienced interviewers are aware of *their* changes or choices mandated by the interviewee and this is used as legitimate information to infer traits or personality constructs. The effect others have on you (to build rapport or find the words to connect with them) is fair game for developing and validating inferences about the interviewee's personality.

Being aware of your own behavioral changes dictated by the style or needs or manner of the interviewee adds much value to the standardized personality information (test) you are also collecting (if qualified). It is advantageous to administer standardized personality instruments especially when the assessment is critical or has high consequences. Professionally sound personality instrumentation is advised and these are not often "the most popular." Professionally sound instruments bring characteristics that other easily obtained (and easy to use) questionnaires do not. Specifically, these instruments demonstrate psychometric properties of reliability (yield consistent results) and validity (typically empirical evidence that the test measures what it intends to measure—that is, psychological traits or constructs). Good personality measures are research based.

Circumstances surrounding the assessment may preclude or affect which personality measure is the best choice but, regardless, semi-structured interviews (a standardized list of questions with embedded open-ended questions) should complement the paper assessment. A few well-regarded personality measures are as follows:

- NEO Personality Inventory
- California Psychological Inventory
- Minnesota Multiphasic Personality Inventory
- Sixteen Personality Factors
- Hogan Personality Inventory

There are strengths and weaknesses to each of the aforementioned measures, but, by far, these tools far outweigh other popular instruments. True personality tests require a level of professional certification by the publisher as well. It is not unusual for the publisher of the test to require a state license as a psychologist to use the measure, for instance. Generally, beware of questionnaires, inventories, or the like that despite their "face valid" appearance offer no technical validation reports. Also "certificates" that can be acquired by attending publisher provided workshops may or may not be accompanied by validity. Sound assessment comes from empirical research not the packaging, workshops, or for that matter, units sold. Caveat emptor.

Select a standardized instrument because it enhances the interview. The instrument will afford "norms" so that you can compare the interviewee against a population (well defined by the publisher) on a trait or construct and this information can further refine interview questions or paths chosen by the interviewer.

For instance, in our "dominant" example earlier, the interviewer rapidly referenced data from a personality inventory and sees that the individual is in the 92nd percentile on dominance, defined by that test as a nasty, pushy, or domineering characteristic where gratification is derived from making others do things (as opposed to experiencing joy from helping others do things together; a socialized or positive power). Along with the additional observations obtained in the first 30 seconds of the interview, the interviewer is well on the way to at least one avenue that requires exploration.

Interpreting personality structure calls for professional guidance. For instance, research suggests that individuals who offer high levels of openness and extraversion and low levels of worry (concern), agreeableness, and conscientiousness (diligence, work ethic) may be ripe for a propensity for risk taking. The utility of personality trait structure depends on the reason for the assessment. Again, on matters of personality assessment, a consultation with a licensed psychologist is advised.

Specific competencies (abilities, characteristics, tendencies, interests, values) are addressed and sample questions are prewritten. There is a pace, a sequence and content is preplanned. However, how the interviewer asks the question and to what extent probes are necessary depend on interview events as they unfold.

Benefits of semi-structured assessment (behavioral interviews that enable freedom to explore, probe, and investigate even if the question is not standardized) in terms of personality assessment are apparent in many fields:

- investigative interviewing
- clinical interviewing
- selection and succession planning
- executive coaching

Multiple methods of assessment, sampling of behavior from many sources, and doing so using different tools enhance the accuracy of personality assessment. If possible, identify responses to scenarios from many aspects of the interviewee's life including work. In the employment arena, certain aspects are legally off-limits and so any assessment done for the making of personnel decisions requires legal training (e.g., American with Disabilities Act, 1990; Title VII Civil Rights Acts, 1964; 1991).

That said, source the individual's thoughts, actions, feelings, and wants based on evidence of past behavior handing life crises, work challenges, or managing themselves in general. Structure the interview strategy so that the areas you probe are predictive of behavior you want in the future or are indicative of the kinds of behaviors you want now.

24. Action Item

Consider carefully the method of recording information from the interview to ensure it is appropriate for the situation (writing notes, typing in, audio-taping, teleconference, or internet records).

Rationale

Interviewers often seek to record information from the interview to be analyzed later. There are different methods of recording this information. Each method brings pros and cons. Weigh the benefits and disadvantages of various options before you select. Consider the utility of recording information, ease of use, and effect on the interviewee and possibly the flow of information and quality of dialogue. Don't reduce information intake (capturing) for the sake of a clean scorecard.

Writing—This method is commonly used for interviews in which the general content, rather than word-for-word responses is needed. Interview guides can be prepared that have space for writing answers between the questions, so the interviewer does not need to flip back and forth between the question guide and his or her notes. This method also allows interviewers to keep comments on the interviewee's tone or other mannerisms that may be important. This method requires fast writing and an ability to write while talking and listening at the same time. Interviewers will often need to decipher their handwriting or rewrite their notes into a format for presentation to others. Interviewees are often comfortable with this method of recording information.

Typing into a laptop or computer—Typing responses directly into a word-processing program often allows interviewers an opportunity to record more information than possible by handwriting and with less intrusiveness than audio or video recordings. This method requires a fast typist who can attend to the interview while typing. In addition, while it is less intrusive, there is often still a barrier between interviewer and interviewee, such as the interviewer facing slightly away to type at a desktop computer, or the physical presence of a laptop computer between interviewer and interviewee.

Audio or video records—Audio or video recording allows the interviewer to have an exact record of the interviewee's responses. The interviewer is able to review the tape later to determine exact responses, and will have the ability to have others witness interviewee's mannerisms or tone. Information from the recordings will often need to be transcribed or summarized. Many interviewees are least comfortable with this type of information recording, and interviewers should be prepared to answer questions regarding where the tapes or records will go and how they will be used.

The Actual Words—When verbatim best reflects content and context, spare others the edit. Editing the words of the interviewee can change everything. Take care not to change the information you collect—sometimes the actual words spoken are best.

25. Action Item

Incorporate self-reflection to fine-tune your assessment acumen.

Rationale

Nondirective counseling techniques advise that more information is collected when you are client centered as opposed to directive. Client-centered interviews can be informative and are valuable assessment tools. The key is to be focused on outcomes so that the questioning process is driven toward a desired outcome—rather than being driven by interviewee preoccupations. Client-centered (or interview-centered) tactics open dialogue and reveal information that might not otherwise be exposed.

Interviewee-centered processes require that the interviewer be nonjudgmental and reflective of what the interviewee says. The interview appears as being driven by the interviewee rather than the interviewer. But, this is only so in order to gain access to the information wanted. The interviewer phrases questions to clarify and reflect:

"You were feeling overwhelmed at the time ..."
"You are saying that you were mistreated ..."
"You are angry ..."
"You need to know more ..."

These clarifying, descriptive responses by the interviewer are powerful mechanisms to trigger additional talking. With a small twist, the interviewer can connect these reflective comments to important factors requiring assessment. For example, in the medical profession, patient-centered interview methods are effective in identifying somatization and its management.

Client-centered interviewing means facilitating understanding of interviewee's needs, interests, concerns, and emotions and integrating these findings into an understanding of the person. Doing this and reflecting it back to the interviewee brings the opportunity to ask additional questions that can be more directive and perhaps useful in terms of the needs of the interviewer. Being interview centered to access more information simply means:

- Place the interviewee's needs first and foremost even before the needs of the interviewer.

Some examples of what this may sound like during a dialogue:

"Tell me more about when you feel that pain ..."
"You are concerned about what could be causing the problem ..."

"You want this position to be something more than we want ..."

"You need to know what would happen after you complete this assignment ..."

"Tell me more about that experience ..."

"You are frustrated, explain to me what that is like for you ..."

Interviewer preoccupation is a common problem in interview situations. You can't focus on your needs while uncovering (or exposing) the needs of someone else. Preoccupation obscures the interviewer's judgment and can lead the interview down an unwanted path. Wrong questions are asked. Listening is diluted. The interviewer disengages.

Distractions of personal interest not germane to the purpose or needs of the interviewer will derail the interview unless these distractions are managed. Reflection and acknowledgment can be used to overcome the barrier of preoccupation in a variety of settings. Reflection and labeling of the distraction or preoccupation can remove this barrier and make accessible information that is needed.

Enter interview settings placing your needs, motives, and wants and desires in its proper place. If they appear and interfere, mentally acknowledge it, "label it" (i.e., "I am focusing on what I need rather than what the interviewee needs; stop pressing and stay in the moment") and dive back into the needs of your interviewee.

Suggested Readings

Action Item 1

Burke, B. L., Arkowitz, H., & Menchola, M. (2003). The efficacy of motivational interviewing: A meta-analysis of controlled clinical trials. *Journal of Consulting and Clinical Psychology 71*, 843–861.

Goodstone, M., & Diamante, T. (1998). Organizational use of therapeutic change: Strengthening multi-source feedback systems through interdisciplinary coaching. *Consulting Psychology Journal 50*, 118–136.

Prochaska, J. O., DiClemente, C. C., & Norcross, J. C. (1992). In search of how people change: Applications to addictive behaviors. *American Psychologist 47*, 1102–1114.

Action Item 2

Diamante, T., & Primavera, L. (2004). The professional practice of executive coaching: Principles, practices and decisions. *International Journal of Decision Ethics 1*, 85–114.

Gifford, R., Ng Fan, C., & Wilkinson, M. (1985). Nonverbal cues in the employment interview: Links between applicant qualities and interviewer judgments. *Journal of Applied Psychology 70*, 729–736.

Action Item 3

Dougherty, T. W., Turban, D. B., & Callender, J. C. (1994). Confirming first impressions in the employment interview: A field study of interviewer behavior. *Journal of Applied Psychology 79*, 659–665.

Gubrium, J. F., & Holstein, J. A. (Eds.) (2002). *Handbook of interview research: Context and method.* Thousand Oaks, CA: Sage Publications.

Schwarz, N. (1999). Self-reports: How the question shapes the answer. *American Psychologist 54*, 93–105.

Action Item 4

Cable, D. M., & Gilovich, T. (1998). Looked over or over-looked? Pre-screening decisions and post-interview evaluations. *Journal of Applied Psychology 83*, 501–508.

Diamante, T. (1993). Unitarian validation of a mathematical problem solving exercise for sales occupations. In F. J. Landy (Ed.), *The Test Validity Yearbook*, a special issue of the *Journal of Business & Psychology 14*, 383–401.

Roberts, W. T., & Higham, P. A. (2002). Selecting accurate statements from the cognitive interview using confidence ratings. *Journal of Experimental Psychology: Applied 8*, 33–43.

Sacket, P. R. (1982). The interviewer as hypothesis tester: The effects of interview impressions of an applicant on question strategy. *Personnel Psychology 35*, 789–801.

Action Item 5

Gifford, R., Ng Fan, C., & Wilinson, M. (1985). Nonverbal cues in the employment interview: Links between applicant qualities and interviewer judgments. *Journal of Applied Psychology 70*, 729–736.

Tromboli, A., & Walker, M. B. (1987). Nonverbal dominance in the communication of affect: A myth? *Journal of Nonverbal Behavior 11*, 180–190.

Young, D. M., & Beier, E. G. (1977). The role of applicant nonverbal communication in the employment interview. *Journal of Employment Counseling 14*, 154–165.

Action Item 6

Eckman, P., & O'Sullivan, M. (1991). Who can catch a liar? *American Psychologist 46*, 913–920.

Frank, M., & Eckman, P. (2004). Appearing truthful generalizes across different deception situations. *Journal of Personality and Social Psychology 86*, 486–495.

McCormack, S. A. (1992). Information manipulation theory. *Communications Monographs 59*, 1–16.

McCormack, S. A. (1997). The generation of deceptive messages: Laying the groundwork for a viable theory of interpersonal deception. In J. O. Greene (Ed.), *Message Production: Advances in communication theory* (pp. 91–126). Mahwah, NJ: Erlbaum.

Action Item 7

Kassin, S. M. (1997). The psychology of confession evidence. *American Psychologist 52*, 221–223.

Vrij, A. (2000). *Detecting lies and deceit: The psychology of lying and the implications for professional practice*. Hoboken, NJ: Wiley.

Action Item 8

Farber, B. A., Bernano, K. C., & Capobianco, J. A. (2004). Clients' perceptions of the process and consequences of self-disclosure in psychotherapy. *Journal of Counseling Psychology 51*, 340–346.

Feigenbaum, W. M. (1977). Reciprocity in self-disclosure within the psychological interview. *Psychological Reports 40*, 15–26.

Murphy, K. C., & Strong, S. R. (1972). Some effects of similarity self-disclosure, *Journal of Counseling Psychology 19*, 121–124.

Action Item 9

Curtis, R., Field, C., Knaan-Kostman, I., & Mannix, K. (2004). What 75 psychoanalysts found helpful and hurtful in their own analyses. *Psychoanalytic Psychology 21*, 183–202.

Lamber, M. J., & Barley, D. E. (2001). Research summary on the therapeutic relationship and psychotherapy outcome. *Psychotherapy 38*, 357–361.

Action Item 10

Mauet, T. A. (2002). *Trial Techniques* (6th ed.), New York, NY: Aspen Publishers.

Wagner Moore, L. E. (2004). Gestalt therapy: Past, present and future, Psychotherapy: theory, research, practice. *Training 41*, 180–189.

Action Item 11

Boxer, D. (2011). The lost art of good schmooze: Building rapport and defusing conflict in everyday and public talk. Westport, CT: Praeger Publishers.

Action Item 12

Bekerian, D. A., & Dennet, J. L. (1993). The cognitive interview. Reviving the issues. *Applied Cognitive Psychology 7*, 275–298.

Colwell, K., Hiscock, C. K., & Memon, A. (2002). Interviewing techniques and the assessment of credibility. *Applied Cognitive Psychology 16*, 287–300.

Diamante, T. (2011). Leadership development programs that work: Individual transformation by design. In London, M. (Ed.), *Handbook of lifelong learning, The Oxford Library of Psychology*. Oxford, UK: Oxford University Press.

Action Item 13

Dipboye, R. L. (1992). *Selection interviews: Process perspectives*. Cincinatti, OH: SouthWestern Publishing.

Schacter, D. L. (1996). *Searching for memory*. New York: Basic Books.

Swann, W. B., & Ely, R. J. (1984). A battle of wills: Self-verification versus behavioral confirmation. *Journal of Personality and Social Psychology 46*, 1287–1302.

Action Item 14

Koehnken, G., Schimossek, E., Aschermann, E., & Hofer, E. (1995). The cognitive interview and the assessment of credibility of adult's statements. *Journal of Applied Psychology 80*, 671–684.

Mann, S., Vrij, A., & Bull, R. (2002). Suspects, lies and videotape: An analysis of authentic high-stake liars. *Law and Human Behavior 26*, 365–376.

Mann, S., Vrij, A., & Bull, R. (2002). Detecting true lies: Police officers' ability to detect suspects' lies. *Journal of Applied Psychology 89*, 137–149.

Action Item 15

Sudman, S. (1982). *Asking Questions*. San Francisco, CA: Jossey-Bass.

Weiss, R. S. (1995). *Learning from strangers: The art and method of qualitative interview studies*. New York, NY: The Free Press.

Action Item 16

Ellis, A. P. J., West, B. J., Ryan, A. M., & DeShon, R. P. (2002). The use of impression management tactics in structured interviews:

A function of question type? *Journal of Applied Psychology 87*, 1200–1208.

Sudman, S. (1982). *Asking Questions*. San Francisco, CA: Jossey-Bass.

Action Item 17

Dunn, J. R., & Schweitzer, M. E. (2005). Feeling and behaving: The influence of emotion on trust. *Journal of Personality and Social Psychology 88*, 736–748.

Ekman, P. (2007). *Emotions revealed*. New York, NY: Henry Holt and Company.

Lazarus, R. S. (1991). *Emotions and adaptation*. New York, NY: Oxford University Press.

Action Item 18

Ekman, P., & Davidson, R. J. (1994). *The nature of emotion: Fundamental questions*. New York, NY: Oxford University Press.

Izard, C. (1977). *Human emotions*. New York, NY: Plenum Press.

Travis, C. (2007). *Anger: The misunderstood emotion*. New York, NY: Simon & Schuster.

Action Item 19

Paunonen, S. V., Jackson, D. N., & Oberman, S. (1987). Personnel selection decisions: Effects of applicant personality and the letter of reference. *Organizational Behavior and Human Decision Processes 40*, 96–114.

Van Iddekinge, C. H., Raymark, P. H., & Roth, P. L. (2005). Assessing personality with a structured employment interview: Construct-related validity and susceptibility to response inflation. *Journal of Applied Psychology 90*, 536–552.

Action Item 20

Huffcutt, A. I., Roth, P. L., & McDaniel, M. A. (1996). A meta-analytic investigation of cognitive ability in employment interview evaluations: Moderating characteristics and implications for incremental validity. *Journal of Applied Psychology 81*, 459–473.

Action Item 21

Brody, N., & Ehrlichman, H. (1998). *Personality psychology: The science of individuality*. New Jersey: Prentice Hall.

Van Iddekinge, C. H., Raymark, P. H., & Roth, P. L. (2005). Assessing personality with a structured employment interview: Construct-related validity and susceptibility to response inflation. *Journal of Applied Psychology 90*, 536–552.

Walsh, W. B., & Betz, N. E. (2001). *Tests and Measurements*. New Jersey: Prentice Hall.

Widiger, T. A., & Samuel, D. B. (2005). Evidence-based assessment of personality disorders. *Psychological Assessment 17*, 278–287.

Action Item 22

Goleman, D. (2006). *Emotional intelligence: Why it can matter more than IQ*. New York, NY: Random House.

Levenstein, J. H. (1989). Patient centered clinical interviewing. In: M. Steward, & D. Roter (Eds.), *Communicating with medical patients* (pp. 107–120). London: Sage Publication.

Smith, C. R. (1991). Somatization disorders: Defining its role in clinical medicine. *Journal of General Internal Medicine 6*, 168–75.

Smith, C. R., et al. (2000). Evidence-based action items for teaching patient-centered interviewing. *Patient Education and Counseling 39*, 27–36.

Action Item 23

Ekman, P. (2009). *Telling Lies: Clues to deceit in the marketplace, politics and marriage*. New York, NY: W.W. Norton & Company.

McCrae, R. R., & Costa, P. T. (1997). Personality trait structure as a human universal. *American Psychologist 52*, 509–516.

Nardone, D. A. (1990). Collecting and analyzing data: Doing and thinking. In H. K. Walker, W. D. Hall & J. W. Hurst (Eds.). *Clinical methods* (pp. 22–28). (3rd edn.) Boston, MA: Butterworth Publication.

Nicholson, N., Soane, E., Fenton-O'Creevy, M., & Willman, P. (2005). Personality and domain-specific risk taking. *Journal of Risk Research 8*, 157–176.

Sitkin, S. B., & Pablo, A. L. (1992). Reconceptualizing the determinants of risk behavior. *Academy of Management Review 17*, 9–38.

Stoeckle, J. D., & Billings, J. A. (1987). A history of history-taking in the medical interview. *Journal of General Internal Medicine 2*, 119–127.

Action Item 24

Eder, R. W., & Harris, M. M. (Eds.) (1999). *The employment interview handbook*. Thousand Oaks, CA: Sage Publications, Inc.

Action Item 25

Cormier, S., Nurius, P. S., & Osborn, C. J. (2009). *Interviewing and change strategies for helpers: Fundamental skills and cognitive-behavioral interventions*. Pacific Cove, CA: Brooks/Cole.

Fontana, A., & Frey, J. H. (2000). The interview: From structured questions to negotiated text. In N. K. Denzin, & Y. S. Lincoln (Eds.). *Handbook of qualitative research*. Thousand Oaks, CA: Sage Publications.

Johnson, D. (2012, May 26). A game to help doctors ask tough questions. *New York Times*, A13.

Rogers, C. (1951). *Client-centered therapy*. New York, NY: Houghton Mifflin Company.

SECTION IV

The Inference Is the Difference

This final section focuses on drawing conclusions on the basis of the information collected. The focus is to safeguard the user of information as we return to the employment context where decisions affect the employment status of the individual being interviewed or assessed (i.e., hiring, promoting, developing readiness for higher-level jobs, and termination or firing). Making inferential leaps based on data collected is not an easy task. The advice in Sections I and II is principally driven to facilitate the making of good selection decisions because the questions are job relevant, objective, and behavioral in nature. Despite the fact that such a structured interview will capture useful (i.e., objective and behaviorally based) information, there remain human elements in the decision-making process that require consideration. This section will reduce the risk of making bad decisions even if you collect good information.

1. Action Item

Average interview evaluations across three or four independent unstructured interviews when it is impossible to design a structured interview protocol.

Rationale

Undoubtedly, interviewers are best served by demonstrating a degree of rigor in determining "competencies" or human requirements demanded by a job through a job analysis or other systematic dissection of what the job entails. The result of such a discovery process enhances the legal defense (i.e., validity) of the process as the interviewer can concoct a standardized, structured list of questions (protocol) that link directly to the job. Structure decreases contamination bred by human perception, judgment, and biases.

That said, for a variety of reasons (e.g., logistics, timing, budget, and lack of buy-in), it might not be possible to build a structured interview. It is not advised that you circumvent the requirement to build a structured, job-related interview; however, in practice, frequently things are done rapidly and it seems that oftentimes interviewing, that is, structuring the interview process, does not get the attention it deserves. While it is true that *if* no adverse impact is produced and/or the interviewer does not violate law (asking an illegal question or giving the impression of being biased and/or in violation of EEO laws), then the interview will not likely lead to legal action. However, an interview void of job-related, behavioral insights will also not likely lead to useful information!

The advice here is to protect yourself from yourself. If you failed to structure the interview, then enhance the evaluation process by getting additional interviewers involved and standardize how you interpret the information you collect by using a behaviorally based, objective scorecard. You will improve the inferences drawn by gathering three or four interviewers and averaging their evaluations across the board.

Apparently, the contamination that can affect evaluations is different depending upon the source. Consequently, multiple interviewers "insulate" the candidate from being overly influenced by the poor judgments or biases of a single interviewer. In addition, the added data from multiple sources can bring incremental value in focusing evaluations on "what matters," avoiding the pitfalls of too little, wrong, or improperly weighed information.

2. Action Item

Use the benchmarks established during preinterview to systematically evaluate candidate capabilities.

Rationale

The best way to avoid misinterpretation or biases is to stay close to the structured protocol built before the interview was conducted. This protocol delineates the competencies required for the job, how they manifest, and what questions can be asked to evaluate the candidate on each competency or job challenge. In addition, scoring criteria should be standardized so that responses to interview questions can be consistently evaluated.

By adhering to a planned mechanism of evaluation, the interviewer can stay on track. Often, characteristics or information unrelated to job requirements can influence the interviewer's judgment. This can occur for both good and bad reasons—therefore, the purpose of the interview and the reason for the assessment must be kept in front of the interviewer's eyes at all times, including the evaluation or decision-making phase. Clearly defined competencies, articulated linkages to job requirements, and behavioral "anchors" or objective indicators of good/bad responses should be used to describe (or evaluate) the interview.

3. Action Item

Gauge reaction time as legitimate content.

Rationale

In addition to verbal and nonverbal communication, a lack of signal is also a signal. Focus your radar on the reaction time of the candidate. Is the response to your question delivered in a "concerned" manner—is there hesitation that is warranted? Is the hesitation confusing? Does it feel a bit too calculating? Are the words too quick—appearing as if the answers are "canned" rather than thoughtful?

Reaction time is a metric that can be used to identify whether the candidate is engaged or is being coy, deceptive, or perhaps expressing fear. While the emotion *per se* is not directly calculable, the inappropriate (or uncomfortable) delay in a response should be noted by the interviewer especially when this delay is unexpected or doesn't make sense given the nature of the question posed. You must gauge the total reaction (content of the answer and context of its delivery) to the question you ask.

Certain questions should be relatively quick and easy to respond to:

- What did you like best about your last job?
- Why are you interested in this job?

Others are more challenging:

- What would you do differently in your career, if you could do it all over again?
- What regrets do you have about your career path?
- How would you define success in this assignment?

Hesitation or silence suggests that you struck a chord and so benefit further by probing. Don't miss that opportunity.

4. Action Item

Capitalize on independent evaluators to enhance judgment.

Rationale

Interviews that are structured (i.e., standardized and behaviorally driven including the scoring criteria) are a better bet than the use of unstructured interviews. That said, collapsing judgments from independent evaluators (using unstructured interviews) can improve the validity or accuracy of even the unstructured approach.

Where panels of interviewers are deployed, it is beneficial to require each individual to prepare their evaluations separately and independently and then enter a consensus meeting arriving on an overall decision based on group discussion. It is a mistake to not benefit (or protect yourself) from independent perceptions. The assessment process is enhanced by imposing structure, behavioral objectivity, and independence into the decision-making process. Panels are no exception to this fact.

The use of independence avoids extreme errors and serves as a check-and-balance system. This is especially useful when the interview's validity or structure is unknown or weak. Numerical averages are sometimes used (instead of group discussions), but this does not enable corrective action to take place when an evaluation is wrong, unsupportable, or is motivated by bias.

5. Action Item

Notice what the person says and does and draw inferences when the interview is over.

Rationale

It is difficult to ask good questions, record responses (verbal and nonverbal), digest all of this, and capture the result in your notes. So don't!

Focus on what the candidate says and does. Note verbal and non-verbal responses. Do not attempt to classify or interpret in the moment as you may miss important incoming information. Looking for the forest while you are still foraging through the trees is not a good idea.

While listening, focus on:

- what was accomplished and the context of the situation or circumstance
- why the task/solution was selected or developed
- how the solution/approach was developed or chosen (criteria, weighing of alternatives)
- the end result and objective outcomes (short term, long term)

When the interview is over, the content and context of the interview can be used collectively to draw inferences about the candidate. It is easier and more accurate to review the information gained from the interview when the interview is over. Perspective is everything—wait until the interview is over to review all the evidence you collect.

6. Action Item

Identify contrivance as a key indicator of deception.

Rationale

Evaluate the interviewees' honesty or willingness to provide truthful answers by focusing on the details offered, the context of speech, and the spontaneity of reaction. Deception is difficult work. An interviewee who is evasive will be working very hard to get points across. The communication is contrived, labor-intensive, and the content of the communication often "trips" the interviewee. Please keep in mind that research reveals that interviewers are not skilled at identifying deception.

In the employment context, where integrity is important and responses to job-relevant questions don't feel just right—the interviewer must rely on probing to verify. This is especially true when the answers seem "canned" or that the interviewee is speaking like a talking powerpoint. Simple tactics like asking for clarification or examples will help determine authenticity. Also, it is useful to repeat a question or ask for additional details on a matter discussed earlier in the conversation. Are the descriptions the same? Incongruities (or differences) in information shared is not a good sign. It is hard to revisit or re-explain a complex situation or circumstance especially when the original depiction was contrived.

For instance:

> "Tell me again, how you were able to gain buy-in from senior management on that global initiative when in the past they were so against it?" It is very hard to remember details, especially when trying to reconstruct (that is, re-create) rather than just describe what actually took place.
>
> "You explained that you have experience driving cultural change initiatives and I know you walked us through a sample process of what it might look like. However, I'm still curious about some of the steps you actually took on a project and how you actually implemented a cultural change plan. Will you please tell me, not in general terms but specifically, the steps you took to drive culture change?"
>
> "Can you please tell me again, about the obstacles you faced? I know we covered this earlier, but I am very interested. Explain to me again the challenges you faced, please."

Rather than viewing this as deception, maybe it is useful to think about re-asking the same (or similar) question as just double-checking. If the first articulation is truthful, re-telling the story should not be too taxing. Offering the repeat as a means for the interviewer to learn more should be flattering and welcomed. "Yes, I'd be delighted to explore my work on that project again. What would you like to know?"

Deceptive answers are generally less detailed, less vivid, and details tend to be presented in same format, even when the question posed requires a different format or description. In other words, the interviewee not wanting to reveal being deceptive lacks spontaneity and offers a rigid, rehearsed oratory, almost regardless of the question posed. It's good to ask questions about the same situation, it should be easy to describe an experience from different angles if the truth is being told.

In contrast, honest responses tend to be spontaneous and detailed. The details of the honest response are colorful, can change (and do), and the additional memories or utterances added as the event or circumstance is shared does not produce inappropriate anxiety. Honest responders often have relatively longer responses and provide spontaneous additions of detail that may or may not be linked to your exact question.

Those practicing deception like to end the interview as soon as possible. If you are feeling pressured to bring closure, you should investigate further. Asking to reiterate information, only from a different angle, places additional pressure that is unwanted and is cognitively demanding. Deceptive people don't like to repeat their performances. It's too hard.

Feel free to ask again when the interviewee's authenticity is suspect.

Say, "I'm not exactly clear on the order of events, can we look at that again ...?"

The deceptive response is a performance. The genuine response is authentic.

Actors make a living bridging this gap. Most cannot make the inauthentic appear authentic.

Deception is taxing, tiring, and often becomes a task that deceivers want to end as soon as possible.

Ask the interviewee for multiple descriptions of the same event. Vary the questions slightly "Tell me about what you saw starting from when you first arrived," "Tell me about what happened starting from the very last thing you remembered." "Tell me what it felt like to be witnessing the event and what made you feel that way?"

Deceptive answers lack consistency. By requiring the interviewee to recall events or provide explanations when you demand minor changes in how the event is presented should not be overwhelming to someone who is being open. It is, however, a difficult task for the interviewee with an agenda. It is hard work to describe an event the same way when temporal changes are requested, emotional color is requested, or the interviewee is requested to describe details of physical objects involved.

When the interviewee is being truthful, recall can vary and details wanted (and not wanted) will be offered. Observing a struggle to "get it right" is cognitively taxing, but it should not evoke irritability or anxiety. The interviewee may ramble or share more than you asked for as they try to reconstruct or share information that might be useful.

Conversely, deceptive statements tend to be shorter in length, are less detailed, and are more carefully phrased. Rigid presentations that are unchanging even when the interviewer asks for a different look or description of the event may indicate deception. Deceptive interview responses do not have additions in detail or other minor, spontaneous changes across multiple descriptions of the same event. The interviewer's task is to enable the interviewee to demonstrate that they are being deceptive. This can be done by:

- Asking multiple open-ended questions, for instance:
    - "Tell me, please how you feel about …?"
    - "Do you think, at times, police officers use unwarranted force?"
    - "How did you first come to know about …"
- Vary how you want the interviewee to respond to the "same question"
    - "Tell me your thoughts about why this took place."
    - "Can you explain what the motive might have been?"
    - "Why do you think this happened?"
- Request details from different angles of the same event
    - "Tell me, again please how that person responded beginning with the first thing you saw."
    - "Can you provide some details on what the people were doing just before the event occurred?"
    - "Describe the scene to me, this time starting from the last thing you remember and work your way back to the beginning."

- ○ "Think about how you felt when this was happening, what were you thinking at the time?"
- Enable the interviewee to wax on the same topic, in different ways
  - ○ "Can women earn respect in the workplace?"
  - ○ "Do you think sexual harassment is something that is getting in the way of business or does it get too much attention?"
  - ○ "What are your views about workplace diversity; so many differences—how does such a mix impact your workplace culture?"

7. Action Item

Do not infer that a poor interview conversation will absolutely translate into poor performance or potential.

Rationale

Keep the goal of the assessment in mind at all times. Are you attempting to measure how articulate the candidate is or are you trying to identify a set of skills, a core capability that (elocution aside) can be transferred to a job, or enable performance in a given situation? Keep your eye on the outcome you want.

There can be many reasons for a bad conversation, including factors related to the interviewer and not the interviewee. For instance, are you sending signals that you are bored, disinterested, or do not want to listen? If so, quick answers are a response to your demand and indicate a perceptive candidate. By contrast, cultural or personality influences may impact how a person responds during an interview. For example, in some cultures, making eye contact with a superior is considered rude. Ask yourself, if performance during an interview translates to the application of skills or competencies needed to be successful. It is conceivable that the electrical engineer you need to hire may need to demonstrate eloquence during the employment interview. Know what you are measuring and not measuring during the interview. Don't confuse the two.

Keep your eye on the ball. Know what and why you are assessing people.

8. Action Item

Don't let a particularly good or bad characteristic creep into judgment on other characteristics.

Rationale

A consistent "error" when evaluating interview results is unwittingly allowing strong ratings on one characteristic to affect judgment on other characteristics. This is referred to as a "halo" effect as in the candidate can do no wrong once viewed preferably on some characteristic.

Alternatively, a poor performance or evaluation on one characteristic can affect rating on other characteristics too. This "devil" or "horns" effect is another source of rater or evaluator error.

It is important to realize that these cognitive mistakes are subtle—they lie below the surface of self-awareness. Consequently, the best defense is offense.

Construct an evaluation process with standardized, behavioral scoring criteria. Multiple raters or evaluators can mitigate decision errors by bringing a check-and-balance effect as can training, using mock interviews and behavioral feedback. Most importantly, the structure of the interview should map nicely to the human requirements (competencies) required to do the job or handle the situation for which you are assessing. This linkage should be obvious in exacting behavioral terms in both question content and standardized scoring criteria.

Stay aware, both during and after the interview, for the halo effect. You can evaluate certain aspects of the individual as terrific and other aspects as "not so good." Use your overall scoring criteria to guide your overall evaluation, again based on the job or situational requirements for success.

9. Action Item

Assess the evidence and not its presentation when the manner of delivery is not relevant to your decision.

Rationale

Interviewers, like people, are influenced by many factors when determining what information they attend to, how they weigh information, and what dynamics they succumb to when making decisions. Research informs us that, in particular, impression tactics used by interviewees do indeed relate to overall evaluations. In general, people are not very good judges of people. We need help.

Interviewees who deploy assertive tactics, self-promotion tactics, and self-ingratiation tactics are judged to be more valuable than interviewees who do not. At first glance this may seem like a good thing. After all, it suggests some degree of personality, interpersonal savvy, and even likeability. The problem as far as assessment is concerned lies in the fact that it is the display or performance of such manipulative or influencing behaviors that is being judged *rather than* underlying constructs or core competencies that in fact are the targets of the assessment.

Practically, the lesson here is that interviewers need to focus on the behaviors of the candidate and not merely on the performance in the moment. Said differently, a candidate might be very humorous (self-ingratiating) and also be very self-confident (self-promotional) in the course of their normal day but do not display this during an interview. Interviewers must stay focused on asking questions that will bring evidence of competencies or skills on the job and beware of the cosmetic display before them. The interviewee's mask will come off when behavioral questions are asked. To repeat a theme—ask what did you do, how did you do it, what was the outcome. The demands of asking behavioral questions will strip the interviewee of the impression management display.

10. Action Item

Avoid gender-role stereotyping; predilections are dangerous.

Rationale

The perception that certain jobs are "more suitable" for certain genders still leaks into evaluations. Often subtle rather than deliberate, this error is not only bad for the hiring organization, but it is also illegal (unless gender-based criteria are established in advance as a Bona Fide Occupational Qualification, see EEOC Uniform Federal Guidelines). Imperceptibly, judgments can be influenced by a hidden metric—"does the person fit" can wrongly be translated into "does the person fit given 'my' understanding of what 'should' fit?" Danger.

Generally, certain jobs still remain attached to genders more so than others, for instance, firefighter and nurse. This can and does lead to sex-based discrimination (Title VII Civil Rights Act violation, 1964, 1991). It also means that assessments are vulnerable to gender-role stereotyping bias. If the interviewer is thinking "unlikely fit" because of the candidate's gender, there is a tendency to ask questions that will justify or support this preconceived notion. Consequently, the interview develops into a hunt for evidence to disqualify the person. We can easily pay attention to things we want to see and ignore contradictory evidence.

In addition, it is worthwhile to realize that "physical attractiveness" and gender can play an inappropriate role in many ways. For instance, during an assessment for a chief public relations officer for a utility company in the northeast, one of four interviewers shared "the candidate was too good looking and so seems cosmetic or phony to me" (this candidate was male). Research has clearly demonstrated that attractiveness can both positively and negatively unduly impact candidate impressions, sometimes depending on the gender typecasting of the job in question. Another example from practice (not research) pertains to evaluating people negatively when there is an inconsistency between the presenting personality and the expectation for a given gender. When men demonstrate effeminate characteristics and women demonstrate traditional male characteristics, we find assessment difficult. Assessments are influenced by the appearance of the person and the disparity between personality and gender-role norms. Generally, the "confusion" or incongruity experienced by the biased interviewer is problematic and the candidate is wrongfully rejected (i.e., typically the overall evaluation of the individual is negative, so the blatant influence of gender-role stereotyping is not apparent). It is worth repeating that the making of decisions on the basis of gender is illegal (unless it qualifies as a BFOQ, see the Uniform Federal Guidelines).

Preinterview work and training minimize mistakes.

Prepare competency models or stipulate demands in concrete, operational terms. Turn these objective statements into a benchmarking scorecards acting as a "guard rail" for the interviewer when evaluating the interviewee.

It is noteworthy that interviewers need to "mind themselves" as apparently those who self-monitor can filter faulty judgments and stay on-track with established evaluative criteria that are gender-neutral and fair to everyone regardless of backgrounds or legally protected characteristics.

11. Action Item

Make decisions against what you can't change, not what you can.

Rationale

When evaluating qualifications, compare assessment results to a stated need. The stated need should be in the form of written, well-defined "competencies"—if possible, within each competency definition provide a manifestation of that competency, in a sense providing an example or justification of why the competency is needed by showing how it contributes to a business or other desirable outcome.

Complementary characteristics need to be weighed against requirements. That is, consider the extent to which a competency can be trained versus identifying it as not trainable. With this in mind, you can prioritize critical competencies that are not trainable and "balance" or decide to train on competencies that can be altered. For example, simple skills can be acquired (e.g., knowledge of fundamental bookkeeping), whereas turning an individual into an "affable" person is not so easily accomplished. Given the need for someone who is excellent with clients, establishing rapport on the phone or in person or otherwise working cooperatively in a small business setting—and relative to the strengths of other candidates interviewed—it makes sense to place the affable candidate and teach them the bookkeeping on the job.

Clarity about business/situational requirements drives the determination of critical versus useful information. It is important to state core requirements and essential competencies needed for the job versus those useful but not necessary essential. Understanding what you are willing to do to "train" or develop candidates will help you establish the criteria you want to use to judge or evaluate the candidates (considering cost, time, urgency, level of expertise). Possibly, you will be making a trade-off of placing an individual who brings one set of assets but is deficient on another set that can be developed.

Will the individual with weak technical skills yet strong on people skills be successful? Are the technical skills trainable? How quickly? At what cost? What are essential functions of the job/situation and what are the nonnegotiable competencies (knowledge, skills, abilities, and personal characteristics) requisite for success?

Evaluate interview results based on established requirements and keep in mind that some competencies you may find useful might require making a trade-off for another competency that is essential.

12. Action Item

Consider the mutuality of the interview process and the potential role of the interview as intervention.

Rationale

Some interviews are structured to merely obtain information from individuals, with assumptions that the information that interviewees provide is accurate and trustworthy. There is often an assumption that the interviewer should function as a neutral individual, a mere fact-gatherer, who does not in any way influence the responses of the interviewee. Yet, in reality, the interview process is an endeavor that is an exchange of information with a duality all its own. In these circumstances, it is possible that individuals may learn from each other, which can lead to new directions during the interview, which is not of course the purpose of an employment interview (which should always be targeted, structured, and remain on-point).

Ethical considerations should also be considered when the interview is a dialogue or a means to an end beyond assessment for purpose of hiring, promotion, or placement. Examples of this would include interviews for a research purpose or interviews for the sake of changing perception or understanding of a topic, a person, or a circumstance, such as during executive coaching.

For sake of clarity and for ethical reasons it is appropriate to address (a) informed consent to ensure that interviewees participate only after fully understanding the process they are agreeing to, (b) right to privacy to protect the interviewee from inappropriate disclosure of information, and (c) protection from harm to ensure that the interviewee is safe from physical or emotional harm during the time that he or she is in care of the interviewer.

Interviews require consideration of ethics and purpose and, when in doubt, err on the side of consent, transparency, and protection from harm.

13. Action Item

Evaluate results considering the method used when asking questions.

Rationale

Quantum physics brought us the "uncertainty principle," which states simply that we can never "know" truth because the very act of observation or measurement alters that truth. This is true of the interview.

Records of what is said and done during the interview are outcomes of an *interaction* rather than a measure of the individual, *per se*. To the extent that interview results reflect interactions, the role of the interviewer is critical. While all aspects of the interviewer's persona interact with the interviewee, here we focus on the method of interviewing as a controllable variable.

Is the interviewer …

- Warm—Cold
- Sensitive—Insensitive
- Engaged—Aloof
- Abrupt—Polite
- Authoritarian—Involving
- Respectful—Condescending
- Genuine—Inauthentic

The interviewer's method can be a reflection of the interviewer's personality. The point here is to deploy interview style as a prompt (or tool). Interviewer style is itself part of the interview—and affects the person with whom you hope to reach.

Always consider the person doing the interview, the nature of the interview, and how questions are levied. Interview results reflect the process of observing the interviewee—interview results are not derived from a vacuous environment. How the interviewer engages the interview affects the outcome of the assessment. Like dipping your toe in a pool to measure temperature, the personality or approach of the interviewer affects what you are trying to measure. Understand how you are taking the temperature of your interviewee so your affect is known.

For example, before the interview started, the interviewer decided he did not like the candidate on the basis of the resume, but nonetheless was required to conduct the interview. The responses born of this interaction reflects more the *interviewer* than the *interviewee*. It is worth noting that biases and assumptions can affect interview results even before a word is spoken. In the employment situation or under human resource decision-making circumstances, biases that are based on race, color, national origin, disability, religious orientation, and other protections can be a cause for legal action.

14. Action Item

Utilize ambivalence to obtain more information during the exchange.

Rationale

Interviewers can impact the interviewee experiencing ambivalence using motivational techniques. A therapeutic tactic called motivational interviewing can be a gentle nudge to interviewees to encourage making better choices and even directing that process. When interviewing for selection or placement of course, the interviewer is not focused on changing or advising the person. Motivational interviewing is a deliberate use of an interview or assessment situation to accelerate behavior change or enhance life decision-making processes.

An astute interviewer can identify a conflict or confusion and inquire in a way that invites more information. Many times, interviewers explore the nature of conflict and can help parse what matters to the person and/or what the individual wants. In so doing, the interviewer accelerates a motivational process so that the individual moves to a point of inflection, where choice and consequence are self-determined.

Interviewers can help identify what may be keeping the interviewee from making a change; that is, they can identify the benefit to the interviewee for maintaining the current behavior and *not* making changes. Once these issues are discovered, the interviewer can then make a summarizing comment, such as the following: "So you're saying that you want to change [situation] because x, y, and z are problems for you, but right now, you're experiencing a and b, which makes it hard for you to take steps to make change." Frequently, this type of interviewing is used to encourage people to change addictive or unproductive behaviors, but reflecting and summarizing can be helpful for many types of changes in work and life.

In assessment situations, motivational interviewing techniques can be employed to look at analytical reasoning, decision-making skills, and critical thinking. When questions are phrased based on job challenges (i.e., job requirements), the question becomes a highway to thought that can be related to a job. "When you were managing the business unit, you chose not to implement a culture change initiative despite the fact that your numbers were terrible. Tell me about how you decided to take a different direction. What did you learn from your decision and in the future, in similar situations, how might you act and why?"

15. Action Item

Make final judgments remembering that interview data not only reflect the candidate, but also you and the interaction between you and the candidate.

Rationale

The human element involved in observing, attending to, interpreting, and evaluating information cannot be overstated. Adhere to (create) a scorecard that anchors judgments in behaviors that were observed.

Respect the fact that interview results reflect an interaction that takes place, when useful, factor that reality into your view of what you heard or witnessed.

Would the results of the interview be different if someone other than you had interviewed the person? What does that mean? What aspects of the person caught your eye immediately? Is the interaction acknowledged in how information is interpreted? What information are you attending to? Ignoring? What did you seek? Avoid?

- Analyze your motivations and make sure you stick to the behavioral scoring criteria so you do not unduly influence the evaluation based on irrelevant factors (i.e., biases).
- Consider biases you bring or extraneous factors influencing the process (e.g., political considerations, needs of the business, pressure to find or not find a characteristic).
- Dig deep for stereotypes, personal biases, or other human factors that might incorrectly influence what you see, record, and utilize to make evaluations.
- Realize that you come to know the result of an interaction rather than the "truth."
- Detect your perceptual filter (personality) and make sure it is working *for* you and not *against* you.

Interviews are dynamic events. Embrace your humanity when evaluating others and aim for a level of understanding, appreciation, and judgment that reflects wisdom about yourself and those you meet.

Suggested Readings

Action Item 1

McDaniel, M. A., Whetzel, D. L., Schmidt, F. L., & Maurer, S. D. (1994). The validity of employment interviews: A comprehensive review and meta-analysis. *Journal of Applied Psychology 79*, 599–616.

Schmidt, F. L., & Zimmerman, R. D. (2004). A counterintuitive hypothesis about employment interview validity and some supporting evidence. *Journal of Applied Psychology 89*, 553–561.

Action Item 2

Handbook of Industrial, Work and Organizational Psychology. (2001). In Anderson, N., Ones, D. S., Sinangil, H. K., & Viswevar, C. (Eds.). *Personnel psychology* (volume 1). Thousand Oaks, CA: Sage Publications.

Reifers, S. (1980). How to avoid bias in interviewing women. *EEO Today. New York 7(3)*, 223.

Action Item 3

Cormier, W. H., & Cormier, L. S. (1991). *Interviewing strategies for helpers: Fundamental skills and cognitive behavioral interventions.* Pacific Grove, CA: Brooks/Cole Publishing.

Thompson, C. B. (2002). *Interviewing techniques for managers.* New York, NY: McGraw Hill.

Action Item 4

Diamante, T. (2009). Authentic performance: The valuation of behavior as a negotiated outcome. In M. London & J. Smither (Eds.). *Performance management. Society for industrial & organizational psychology: Professional practice series.* New York, NY: John Wiley.

Raza, S. M., & Carpenter, B. N. (1987). A model of hiring decisions in real employment interviews. *Journal of Applied Psychology 72*, 596–603.

Action Item 5

Kacmar, K. M., Delery, J. E., & Ferris, G. R. (1992). Differential effectiveness of applicant impression management tactics on employment interview decisions. *Journal of Applied Social Psychology 29*, 1250–1272.

Peters, L. H., & Terborg, J. R. (1975). The effects of temporal placement of unfavorable information and of attitude similarity on personnel decisions. *Organizational Behavior and Human Performance 13*, 279–293.

Action Item 6

Colwell, K., Hiscock, C. K., & Memon, A. (2002). Interviewing techniques and the assessment of credibility. *Applied Cognitive Psychology 16*, 287–300.

DePaulo, B. M., & Kashy, D. A. (1998). Everyday lies in close and casual relationships. *Journal of Personality and Social Psychology 74*(1), 63–79.

DePaulo, B. M., Lindsay, J. L., Malone, B. E., Muhlenbrock, L., Charlton, K., & Cooper, H. (2003). Cues to deception. *Psychological Bulletin 129*, 74–118.

Eckman, P., & O'Sullivan, M. (1991). Who can catch a liar? *American Psychologist 46*, 913–920.

Action Item 7

Daniel, C., & Valencia, S. (1991). Structured interviewing simplified. *Public Personnel Management 20*, 127–134.

Action Item 8

Fontana, A., & Frey, J. H. (2000). The interview: From structured questions to negotiated text. In N. K. Denzin & Y. S. Lincoln (Eds.). *Handbook of qualitative research*. Thousand Oaks, CA: Sage Publications.

London, M. (Ed.) (2001). *How people evaluate others in organizations*. Mahwah, NJ: Erlbaum Associates.

Miller, W. R., Rollnick, S., & Conforti, K. (2002). *Motivational interviewing*. New York, NY: Guilford Press.

Action Item 9

Dearnley, C. (2005). A reflection on the use of semi-structured interviews. *Nurse Researcher. Interviewing 13*, 19–28.

Kvale, S. (1996). *Interviews: An Introduction to qualitative research interviewing.* London: Sage.

Action Item 10

Arvey, R., & Campion, J. (1982). The employment interview: A summary and review of recent research, *Personnel Psychology 35*, 281–322.

Barrick, M. R., Patton, G. K., & Haughland, S. N. (2000). Accuracy of interviewer judgments of job applicant personality traits. *Personnel Psychology 53*, 925–951.

Ryan, A. M., & Sackett, P. R. (1989). Exploratory study of individual assessment practices: Inter-rater reliability and judgments of assessor effectiveness. *Journal of Applied Psychology 74*, 568–579.

Silzer, R., & Jenneret, R. (2011). Individual psychological assessment: A practice and science in search of common ground. *Industrial and Organizational Psychology 4*, 270–296.

Action Item 11

Ellis, A. P. J., West, B. J., Ryan, A. M., & DeShon, R. (2002). The use of impression management tactics in structured interviews: A function of question type. *Journal of Applied Psychology 87*, 1200–1208.

Godfrey, D. K., Jones, E. E., & Lord, C. G. (1986). Self-promotion is not ingratiating. *Journal of Personality and Social Psychology 50*, 106–115.

Higgins, R. L., Snyder, C. R., & Berglas, S. (1990). *Self-handicapping: The paradox that isn't.* New York, NY: Plenum Press.

Action Item 12

Davidson, H. K., & Burke, M. J. (2000). Sex discrimination in simulated employment context: A meta-analytic investigation. *Journal of Vocational Behavior 56*, 225–248.

Jawahar, I. M., & Mattsson, J. (2005). Sexism and beautyism effects in selection as a function of self-monitoring level of decision-maker. *Journal of Applied Psychology 90*, 563–573.

Schein, V. E. (1973). The relationship between sex role stereotypes and requisite management characteristics. *Journal of Applied Psychology 57*, 95–100.

Uniform Federal Action Items on Employee Selection Procedures. (1978). 29 Code of Federal Regulations, Part 1607.

Action Item 13

Diamante, T. (2011). Leadership development programs that work: Individual transformation by design. In M. London (Ed.). *Handbook of lifelong learning, The Oxford Library of Psychology.* UK: Oxford University Press.

Dipboye, R., & Gaugler, B. (1993). Cognitive and behavioral processes in the selection interview. In N. Schmitt & W. C. Borman (Eds.). *Personnel selection in organizations.* San Francisco, CA: Jossey-Bass.

Wexley, K. N., Yukl, G. A., Kovacs, S. Z., & Sanders, R. E. (1972). Importance of contrast effects in employment interviews. *Journal of Applied Psychology 56*, 45–58.

Ziegert, J. C., & Hanges, P. J. (2005). Employment discrimination: The role of implicit attitudes, motivation and a climate for racial bias. *Journal of Applied Psychology 90*, 553–562.

Action Item 14

Dipboye, R., & Gaugler, B. (1993). Cognitive and behavioral processes in the selection interview. In N. Schmitt & W. C. Borman (Eds.). *Personnel selection in organizations.* San Francisco, CA: Jossey-Bass.

Wexley, K. N., Yukl, G. A., Kovacs, S. Z., & Sanders, R. E. (1972). Importance of contrast effects in employment interviews. *Journal of Applied Psychology 56*, 45–58.

Ziegert, J. C., & Hanges, P. J. (2005). Employment discrimination: The role of implicit attitudes, motivation and a climate for racial bias. *Journal of Applied Psychology 90*, 553–562.

Action Item 15

Gorassini, D., Harris, J. A., Diamon, A., & Flyn-Dastoor, E. (2006). Computer assessment of interrogative suggestibility. *Personality and Individual Differences 40*, 569–577.

Kurtz, M. A. (2007). *Interviewee perceptions of group interaction in an employment interview.* South Dakota: South Dakota State University.

Rabon, D. (2008). *Interviewing and interrogation.* Durham, NC: Carolina Academic Press.

Schmitt, N. (1976). Social and situational determinants of interview decisions: Implications for the employment interview. *Personnel Psychology 29*, 79–101.

Index

A

ADA. *See* Americans with Disabilities Act
Age Discrimination in Employment Act (1967), 27
Altruism, 99
Ambivalence, 132–133
Americans with Disabilities Act (ADA), 27, 44, 55–56
Aptitude, 62
Asking questions, methods used for, 131–132
Assess authenticity, 80–81
Assess core success characteristics, 61–63
Assess intelligence, 100–102
Assessment
  authenticity, 80–81
  core success characteristics, 61–63
  evidence, 126–127
  intelligence, 100–102
  specialists, 61
Assessment specialists, 61
Avatar-type interview processes, 26
Average interview evaluations, 117–118

B

Behavioral "anchors," 12, 13
Behavioral description interviews, 21
Behavioral evaluation standards, 12
Bias, avoidance, 41–42
Big Five factors, 99
Body language, interviewer, 79–80

C

Candidate capabilities, evaluation, 118–119
Characteristic creep, 126
Civil Rights Act (1964, 1991), 27
Client-centered interviewing, 107
Cognitive ability, 41, 100–102
Common interviewer errors, 56–57
Common mistakes, 42
Communicate accountability, 53
Communication barriers, overcome, 42–44
Competencies, 14, 19, 129
Competency modeling, 2
Competency-relevant information, 48
Competent communication, 42
Complementary characteristics, 129
Computerized interviews, 25–26
Conduct intense assessments, 82–84
Continuous learning orientation, 62
Contrivance, 121–125

D

Decisions, 45
Demonstrate patience, 88–89

E

Emotional expressions, 97–98
Emotional intelligence, 101
Employment interview questions, 9, 10
Employment interviews, 3, 19
Encourage disclosure, 84–85
Engaged interviewees, 85
Equal Employment Opportunity (EEO), 15, 28
Equal Employment Opportunity Commission (EEOC), 55
Equal Employment Opportunity Laws, 27
Evidence, assess, 126–127
Expansiveness, 62

F

Facts, obtaining, 94–95
Final judgments, interview, 133–134

G

Gauge reaction time, 119–120
Gender-role stereotyping, 127–129

H

"Halo" effect, 126
Healthy interpersonal springboard, 74
Hiring and promotion interviews, 2
Hiring rates, 19
Human competencies, 28
"Humane" treatment, 26
Hypothetical questions, 21

I

Immigration Reform and Control Act (1986), 27
Incorrect inferences, 7
Independent evaluators, capitalize, 120
Inferences, interview, 121
Information evaluation, 31–32
Information gathering, 96
Interplay, interview, 39
Interview content, 4, 11
Interview conversation, 125
Interview data, 51
Interview dimensions, 12
Interviewee actions, 23
Interviewee-centered processes, 107
Interviewer preoccupation, 108
Interview, length of time, 54
Interview outcomes improvement, 85–86
Interview performance, 46
Interview process, preparation for, 1
Interviews. *See also* specific interviews
  contextual factors about, 73
  information at beginning of, 74
Interview situations, 8
Interview structure, 10–11

J

Job analysis, 2–3, 10
Job, essential requirements of, 55

K

Knock-out factors, 19

L

Leadership potential, 24
Legal or regulatory violations, 15
Loose interviews, 49

M

Mutuality and potential role, interview process, 130–131

N

Negative information, nurture, 91–92
Nonsystematic bias, 42
Nonverbal communication, 51
Nonverbal cues, 50–53

O

Objective third party, 30–31
Omniscience, 92
Onus, 2, 47, 51, 65, 77
Open-ended questions, ask, 95–96
Openness, 87–88
"Oral board," 49–50
Orderly progression, 97
Organizational decision makers, 44

P

Panel interviews, 20
Paralanguage, 51
Personal beliefs, analyzes, 63–64
Personal biases, 64
Personality assessment, 102
Personality measures, 98–99
Personnel decision-making tools, 30
Physiognomy, 42
Pregnancy Discrimination Act (1978), 28
Pre-interview impressions, 45–47
Prescreen interviews, 19
Prewritten interview protocol, 78
Probe questions, 57
"Process focus," interview, 45

Q

Question content, 8–9
Quirks or biases, 44–45

R

Rationale behind actions or desires, 57–58
Recording information, method of, 105–106
"Reliability," 1–2
Resilience, 62

S

Scorecards, 32
Scoring key, 1
Scoring standards, 12
Selection interview, 7, 28
Selection practices, 10
Self-awareness, 63
Self-discipline, 99
Self-report personality tests, 99
"Similar to me" effect, 58–59
Sincerity, 83
Situational interview, 21–22
Situational interview questions, 64
Situational responses, 23
Situational specificity, 40
Skilled interviewers, 76, 89
Social settings impact behavior, 7
Solicited team members, 13
Specific errors, avoidance, 48–50
Standardized professional instrumentation, 102–105
Structured interview, 78
Structured interviewer, 12
Structured interview protocol, 16
Style congruent, ask questions in, 59–61
Successful job performance, essential characteristics, 18

T

Technical validation practices, 19
Technical *vs.* nontechnical competencies, 3
Title VII of Civil Rights Act (1964; 1991), 26
"Trial balloons," floating of, 50

U

Uncover self-image, 93–94
Understanding rationale, 58
Uniform Federal Guidelines on Employee Selection Procedures, 18
Uniform Guidelines, 15
Untruthful communications, 80
Unusual questions, 29–30

V

Valid interview, 1
"Validity," 1–2
Value of various answers, 14
VEVRAA. *See* Vietnam Era Veterans' Readjustment Assistance Act of 1974
Vietnam Era Veterans' Readjustment Assistance Act of 1974 (VEVRAA), 28
Vulnerability, 99

OTHER TITLES IN HUMAN RESOURCE MANAGEMENT AND ORGANIZATIONAL BEHAVIOR COLLECTION

Jean Phillips and Stan Gully, Rutgers University, Collection Editors

- *Manage Your Career: 10 Keys to Survival and Success When Interviewing and on the Job* by Vijay Sathe
- *Culturally Intelligent Leadership: Leading Through Intercultural Interactions* by Mai Moua
- *Letting People Go: The People-Centered Approach to Firing and Laying Off Employees* by Matt Shlosberg
- *The Five Golden Rules of Negotiation* by Philippe Korda
- *Cross-Cultural Management* by Veronica Velo
- *Conversations About Job Performance: A Communication Perspective on the Appraisal Process* by Michael E. Gordon and Vernon Miller
- *How to Coach Individuals, Teams, and Organizations to Master Transformational Change: Surfing Tsunamis* by Stephen K. Hacker
- *Managing Employee Turnover: Dispelling Myths and Fostering Evidence-Based Retention Strategies* by David Allen and Phil Bryant
- *Mastering Self-Motivation: Bringing Together the Academic and Popular Literature* by Michael Provitera
- *The Internationalists: Masters of the Global Game* by Catherine W. Scherer
- *Essential Concepts of Cross-Cultural Management: Building on What We All Share* by Lawrence A. Beer
- *Strategy and Training: Making Skills a Competitive Advantage* by Philippe Korda
- *Intercultural Communication for Managers* by Michael Goodman

Announcing the Business Expert Press Digital Library

Concise E-books Business Students Need for Classroom and Research

This book can also be purchased in an e-book collection by your library as
- a one-time purchase,
- that is owned forever,
- allows for simultaneous readers,
- has no restrictions on printing, and
- can be downloaded as PDFs from within the library community.

Our digital library collections are a great solution to beat the rising cost of textbooks. e-books can be loaded into their course management systems or onto student's e-book readers.

The **Business Expert Press** digital libraries are very affordable, with no obligation to buy in future years. For more information, please visit **www.businessexpertpress.com/librarians**. To set up a trial in the United States, please contact **Adam Chesler** at *adam.chesler@businessexpertpress.com* for all other regions, contact **Nicole Lee** at *nicole.lee@igroupnet.com*.

www.ingramcontent.com/pod-product-compliance
Lightning Source LLC
Chambersburg PA
CBHW070550170426
43201CB00012B/1786